BRÉBEUF'S GHOST

BRÉBEUF'S GHOST

a tale of horror in three acts

Daniel David Moses

TORONTO

Exile Editions

2000

This edition is published by Exile Editions Limited,
20 Dale Avenue, Toronto, Ontario, Canada   M4W 1K4

Sales Distribution:
McArthur & Company
c/o Harper Collins
1995 Markham Road
Toronto, ON
M1B 5M8
toll free:
1 800 387 0117
(fax) 1 800 668 5788

Layout and Design by *TIM HANNA*
Composed and Typeset at *MOONS OF JUPITER, INC.* (Toronto)
Printed and Bound by Imprimerie Gauvin
Author's Photograph by *JOHN REEVES*

The Canada Council
Conseil des Arts du Canada

ONTARIO ARTS
COUNCIL

CONSEIL DES ARTS
DE L'ONTARIO

The publisher wishes to acknowledge
the assistance toward publication of
the Canada Council and the Ontario Arts Council.

ISBN 1-55096-529-8

MIX
Paper
FSC® C100212

Can you picture what will be,
so limitless and free,
desperately in need of some stranger's hand
in a desperate land?

The End
— Jim Morrison

The end of the world is at hand. Hello, paleface.

Angels in America, Part Two, Perestroika
— Tony Kushner

Brébeuf's Ghost was produced at the Essex Hall Theatre from 29 May - 1 June, 1996, by the author and by the Department of English and the School of Dramatic Art of the Faculty of Arts at the University of Windsor with the following cast:

JOSEPH	Carlos Velis
PIERRE	Cory O'Brien
the **GHOST**	Mark Lefebvre
BEAR	Matt Harsant
Thunder **VOICE**	John Gray
Fire **CLOUD**	Tom McHale
IRON Man	Rob Duxter
SAMUEL Argent	Michael O'Connor
Sky **FEATHER**	Erinn Eastman
FATHER Noel	Ken MacDougall
THISTLE	Sandra Miller
HAIL Stone Woman	Elana Post
Black **STAR**	Sean D'hondt
Star **LILY**	Dawn Sadler
FLOOD Woman	Monica Côté
a **MOHAWK** warrior	Andy Pogson
a **SECOND** Mohawk warrior	Carlos Velis
a **THIRD** Mohawk warrior	Andy Pogson
a **WARRIOR** of the Sturgeon River Ojibwa	Darren Sims

Directed by *Colin Taylor*
Set by *David Court*
Lighting by *Tedfred Myers*
Costumes by *Katherine Van der Steene*
Stage managed by *Lisa Soda*

CHARACTERS

(in order of appearance)

JOSEPH, a Huron convert

PIERRE, an acolyte

the GHOST

BEAR, Black Star's son, a boy

Thunder VOICE, Fire Cloud's son, a young warrior

Fire CLOUD, a Chief of the Lake Nipissing Ojibwa

IRON Man, a warrior

SAMUEL Argent, a young French trader

Sky FEATHER, Fire Cloud's daughter

FATHER Noel, a Black Robe missionary to the Lake Nipissing
  Ojibwa

THISTLE, Fire Cloud's wife, a convert christened 'Martha'

HAIL Stone Woman, Iron Man's second wife

Black STAR, a shaman

Star LILY, Iron Man's daughter from his first marriage, crippled
  from birth

FLOOD Woman, Iron Man's daughter

North Star, Iron Man's son, a babe in arms

a MOHAWK warrior

a SECOND Mohawk warrior

a THIRD Mohawk warrior

a WARRIOR of the Sturgeon River Ojibwa

Broken Moon, Sky FEATHER's daughter, a babe in arms

SETTING

The rivers and lakes, rocks and shores of the forests of the Canadian Shield between Georgian Bay, Lake Nipissing, and Lake Temagami in central Ontario, first in October 1649 and then in April and then June 1650.

ACT ONE

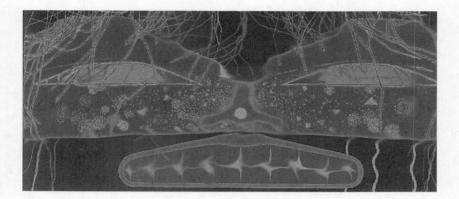

Scene One

The new moon. The calm before freeze-up. In a canoe adrift on Georgian Bay, JOSEPH watches and PIERRE sleeps. PIERRE wakes up suddenly.

JOSEPH: Brother, what's wrong?

PIERRE: Something bit me.

JOSEPH: A black fly.

PIERRE: I thought the frost got them all.

JOSEPH: It never gets all of them. Go back to sleep. You need to rest. It's a long day tomorrow.

PIERRE: I hate to close my eyes. All I see is Sainte Marie.

JOSEPH: You need to be ready when he comes. I'll keep watching.

PIERRE: Listen to me, Joseph.

JOSEPH: What is it, brother?

PIERRE: He won't come. Not now.

JOSEPH: He gave us his word.

PIERRE: Joseph, you know what happened.

JOSEPH: Have you lost your faith?

PIERRE: My poor Joseph.

JOSEPH: Then sleep. I've got better eyes than you do. Huron eyes. I'll see him first. Lie back down.

PIERRE: All my eyes dream are the fire and smoke rising up the spire of the church.

Clouds cover the moon.

JOSEPH: Fire and smoke rising up to heaven. Soon we won't need any more dreams.

PIERRE: Joseph, my brother—

JOSEPH: Quiet, Pierre!

PIERRE: What?

JOSEPH: I hear it.

PIERRE: What is it? I don't hear anything.

JOSEPH: I hear his voice!

PIERRE: That hum? It's those damned black flies, Joseph.

JOSEPH: No. Listen. It's him.

PIERRE: Father Brébeuf?

JOSEPH: Singing! Singing to the glory of our God!

PIERRE: Are the Iroquois torturing him, mocking him on the cross?

JOSEPH: No. I'm not dreaming, not asleep. I hear him now. He's coming.

The GHOST enters in a cloud of black flies.

JOSEPH: Praise be to the Lord of the sky, he is risen!

PIERRE: Holy Jesus!

JOSEPH: Yes, he walks on the water like our Saviour holy Jesus did.

PIERRE: Witchcraft!

JOSEPH: Brother, don't cry.

PIERRE: But it's witchcraft, Joseph.

JOSEPH: It's Father Brébeuf.

PIERRE: No, it's their devil work.

JOSEPH: He's kept his word, Pierre.

PIERRE: The flies, brother, the flies!

JOSEPH: Cover yourself. He's fighting the devil.

PIERRE: Then the devil reeks!

JOSEPH: Have faith.

PIERRE: What's he saying? Why's he looking at me that way?

JOSEPH: He wants us to follow him. *(he picks up his paddle)*

PIERRE: His skin—

JOSEPH: He wants us to follow him!

PIERRE: It's peeling off him!

JOSEPH: Fishers of men, Pierre, fishers of men!

PIERRE: I'm afraid.

JOSEPH: Have faith, Pierre! Pick it up. The end of the world is at hand. Pick up your paddle!

> *PIERRE picks up his paddle. The GHOST turns and exits. JOSEPH and PIERRE start to paddle, following him. Thunder and lightning.*

Scene Two

A rainy day. A hunting camp south of the mouth of the French River on Georgian Bay. BEAR sleeps by the fire. Thunder VOICE enters into the shelter of the lean-to and pours a cup of tea from one of the pots on the coals.

VOICE: Hey boy, wake up. You make this piss?

BEAR: It's from this morning.

VOICE: Cold as the rain. Start packing up the canoes.

BEAR: Why you back so soon?

VOICE: We're going home.

BEAR: Did they get a moose?

VOICE: Get to work.

BEAR: Where's my father? What happened?

VOICE: Can't you see? Your old man says you can see.

BEAR: Where is he?

VOICE: You can't see shit.

BEAR: 'Thunder Voice'! 'Thunder Voice'? What kind of name is that?

VOICE: You leave my name alone.

BEAR: It doesn't mean much.

VOICE: Little boy, little 'old man', I'm not afraid of you.

BEAR: I mean, it's strange, strange,—

VOICE:	Shut up.
BEAR:	—but I can't hear you speak.
VOICE:	You're not your father.
BEAR:	'Thunder Voice'?
VOICE:	You sit here tending the fire like a woman.
BEAR:	No, sounds more like the Black Robe's fart.
VOICE:	Hear this!
BEAR:	Let me go!
VOICE:	Don't you ever threaten me!
BEAR:	Let go! You smell like his farts too!
VOICE:	Your medicine is old and weak.
BEAR:	Your sister doesn't think so.
VOICE:	You leave my sister alone.
BEAR:	Tell her to leave me alone. Use your black robe medicine. Make her behave herself.
VOICE:	Get away from me.
CLOUD:	*(off)* Boy!
VOICE:	Little boy, you better watch yourself this winter.
CLOUD:	*(off)* Come help the Frenchman up the path!
BEAR:	A Frenchman?
CLOUD	*(off)* Do you hear me?

VOICE: Hiding on the beach.

BEAR: Alone?

VOICE: Pale as a crayfish.

CLOUD: *(off)* Hey, boy, come here right now!

BEAR: Your father's calling you.

VOICE: I'll go when I'm ready.

BEAR: Another Black Robe?

VOICE: No, little boy, a man. A trader.

CLOUD: *(entering)* What are you doing there, boy? Go help bring the Frenchman over the rocks.

VOICE: Let him help himself.

CLOUD: He's weak. We have to protect him.

VOICE: Are we supposed to carry him all the way home?

CLOUD: Black Star says—

VOICE: Why do we always do what that old man says?

CLOUD: Show respect.

VOICE: He never brings us any meat. Let Iron Man help him.

CLOUD: Go. Now.

BEAR: The Black Robe will want to see a Christian.

CLOUD: Do as you're told.

BEAR: So will your mother.

VOICE: Little boy, you watch yourself. *(he exits)*

CLOUD: What did you say?

BEAR: Nothing.

CLOUD: He's angry.

BEAR: He's always angry.

CLOUD: Don't look at me that way. Your father should teach you manners.

BEAR: I'm sorry.

CLOUD: My son, he won't bother you anymore.

BEAR: Where is my father?

CLOUD: He had to go south. He'll meet us at the village.

BEAR: He had to go south?

CLOUD: He said something was coming.

BEAR: Is it the dream? It was a powerful dream. I think he's too old to stop it.

CLOUD: You'd better be wrong.

BEAR: It rained a lot at the start of the dream. All the animals ran away and hid.

CLOUD: Your father's a great and powerful man. We'll get a moose on the way home.

Thunder VOICE and IRON Man enter, supporting SAMUEL Argent.

IRON: Where do you want him?

BEAR: By the fire.

IRON: He's heavy as shit.

They drop SAMUEL Argent and he curls up beside the fire.

VOICE: He smells like shit too. They all do.

CLOUD: Start on the canoe.

VOICE: Can't we wait till the rain lets up?

CLOUD: There's no time. Black Star said it'll last three more days.

VOICE: He doesn't know that.

IRON: The Iroquois burned the Huron villages down.

BEAR: That's where the Black Robes are?

IRON: That's what the Frenchman says.

VOICE: Why should we believe what he says either?

IRON: He was with the Black Robes. It's what you and my daughter saw from the dreamer's rock, isn't it? When your father sent the two of you up there in the summer?

VOICE: Why should we believe this? He's a child.

CLOUD: Why can't you do as you're told?

VOICE: Is this a way for grown men to act?

CLOUD: You're the one who whines like a brat.

VOICE: Father Noel could make this rain stop. He would pray to his god.

CLOUD: Take my rifle. Take it to our canoe.

VOICE: I don't want to get wet.

Fire CLOUD slaps Thunder VOICE.

VOICE: It's not my fault if it rusts. *(he takes the rifle and exits)*

IRON Man rolls up his bedding and exits.

CLOUD: The Frenchman, he hasn't eaten for days.

BEAR: There's some banic and fish from this morning.

CLOUD: Get it for him. *(he starts to pack)* Your father said you better be the one to take care of him.

BEAR takes the food to SAMUEL Argent.

BEAR: Here, Frenchman. Wake up. He looks sick.

CLOUD: Make sure he eats. *(he exits with a load)*

BEAR: *(helping SAMUEL sit up)* Come on, chew on this. I'll get you some tea.

SAMUEL: *(eating)* What's his name? That bad boy who won't do as he's told?

BEAR: You speak our language?

SAMUEL: A little. I come here to trade. I learn enough to trade.

BEAR: His name's Thunder Voice.

SAMUEL: It must be a baby thunder. And what do they call you?

BEAR: Eat up.

SAMUEL: My name's Samuel.

BEAR: We got a couple of long days ahead of us.

SAMUEL: One of the Black Robes told me Samuel means 'the name of the Great Spirit'.

BEAR: You shouldn't tell me that.

SAMUEL: Why not?

BEAR: You don't know who I am. I could use your name to hurt you.

SAMUEL: No, I don't think so. I know who you are.

Scene Three

In the rainy night in a wigwam in the village at the mouth of the La Vase River on the east shore of Lake Nipissing, FATHER Noel kneels down alone to pray.

FATHER: Soul of Christ, sanctify me. Body of Christ, save me.

Sky FEATHER, cloaked against the rain in a trade blanket, enters, hurrying along the path past the wigwam.

FATHER: Blood of Christ, exalt me. Water from the side of Christ, wash me.

Sky FEATHER stops to listen for a moment, then exits.

FATHER: My good Jesus, hear me. Within your wounds hide me. Never permit me to be separated from you. At the hour of death, call me. And bid me—

An unearthly howl in the night. FATHER Noel crosses himself, gets to his feet and steps out into the night.

FATHER: Who's there? Father? Father Brébeuf, is it you?

The GHOST enters, wounds full of maggots.

FATHER: *(falling to his knees:)* Oh, Father, what have they done to you? Where is your beard, Father? Where is your tongue? What are you saying, Father? I can't understand you.

The unearthly howl.

FATHER: I'm so sorry. Oh Father, don't cry. Don't look at me that way. Don't. Don't!

Thunder and lightning. FATHER Noel falls prostrate on the ground. The GHOST exits. Sky FEATHER re-enters and finds FATHER Noel in the path.

FEATHER: Mother! Mother, come here

THISTLE: *(off)* What is it? I'm trying to pray!

FEATHER: Mother!

THISTLE: *(entering)* Can't you be quiet? What are you doing out here?

FEATHER: I had to pee, all right?

THISTLE: Father? Father Noel?

FEATHER: Mother, don't touch him.

THISTLE: Help me with him.

FEATHER: What's he doing?

HAIL Stone Woman enters.

THISTLE: He's getting wet.

FEATHER: Is he making medicine?

HAIL: What's going on?

THISTLE: He fell down.

FEATHER: He sneaks around in the night and can't see his own feet!

HAIL: Did you make him angry?

THISTLE: Help me with him.

HAIL: Did you take him his food?

FEATHER: I gave him his food.

HAIL: If he's angry, he'll use his medicine against us.

THISTLE: He's praying.

HAIL: It's weak medicine but—

THISTLE: He's asking God for help!

HAIL: Listen to him. There are bad spirits in him.

FEATHER: Mother! Mother, don't touch him.

THISTLE: Father?

FATHER: Martha? Is that you?

THISTLE: Father, can you stand up?

HAIL: Hey, Black Robe!

THISTLE: You're getting wet out here.

HAIL: Black Robe, is that you?

FATHER: Hello, Hail Stone Woman.

HAIL: Are you drunk on communion wine?

THISTLE: Show respect, woman.

FATHER: Father Brébeuf came to me, Martha.

THISTLE: The good Father from Sainte Marie?

FATHER: Like an angel at the end of time.

HAIL: What are they talking about?

FATHER: He brought me news, Martha, good news for all of God's lambs. This is the time, Martha, the time when the son of God will return to take all his children up to heaven.

THISTLE: Praise be, Father.

FEATHER: My father should be here.

FATHER: It will be a time of great trouble, Martha. But he will protect us. He will lead us into the fray.

HAIL: Black Robe, what are you talking about?

FATHER: Devils will inhabit the earth. The gates of hell will open like mouths crying out for blood. But the church we have built here between us with our baptism will save us.

THISTLE: Bless me, Father, for I have sinned.

FEATHER: Why doesn't he just pull her skirt up and get it over with?

THISTLE: Daughter, where are you going?

FATHER: We are His soldiers here on earth.

THISTLE: You got to be baptised now.

FATHER: We will suffer the tortures of the flesh.

HAIL: Are the Iroquois coming? Is that it?

Sky FEATHER exits.

HAIL: Is that what he means?

THISTLE: She has to be baptised.

FATHER: But we will reap our reward.

HAIL: Is it that dream Star Lily and the old man's son had?

FATHER: We will fly up to heaven on wings of fire. Our blood will flow from our veins like rivers and nourish the trees.

THISTLE: Father, my daughter, she isn't saved. She isn't saved. What will I do?

FATHER: There's still time. Let's pray for her. Come. It's raining. She'll find her way.

FATHER Noel and THISTLE move into the shelter of his wigwam. HAIL Stone Woman follows them to the doorway.

FATHER: Kneel down with me, Martha.

THISTLE: Yes, Father.

FATHER: Let us pray.

THISTLE: Yes, Father.

HAIL: What are you doing? Is this that baptising thing?

FATHER &
THISTLE: Our Father Who art in Heaven, Hallowed be your name! May your kingdom come! May your will be done on Earth as it is in Heaven! Give us this day our daily bread. And forgive us...

Black STAR enters, followed by Sky FEATHER.

FEATHER: What happened?

STAR: Nothing. Let me by.

FEATHER: Your son's not with you?

HAIL: You look cold.

FEATHER: What about the rest of the men?

HAIL: Something's wrong with you.

STAR: My son, he's not here? Aren't the other men back?

FEATHER: No. No one's come back.

STAR: No one?

HAIL: You were fighting something bad.

STAR: Let me go to my bed.

HAIL: No, come to my house. No, come on. Star Lily told me to make you my medicine.

STAR: What day is it?

FEATHER: The moon will be full in two days.

HAIL: If this rain ever stops.

STAR: It'll stop tonight.

HAIL Stone Woman enters her wigwam where her infant son North Star and her daughter FLOOD Woman are asleep. Her step-daughter, Star LILY is awake.

LILY: I can feel the frost already.

HAIL: I'll build up the fire.

STAR: I left them two days ago. They should be here!

          Black STAR and Sky FEATHER enter the wigwam.

LILY: They'll be here tomorrow.

FEATHER: Now that the rain's ending. My brother hates travel-
          ling in the wet!

HAIL: Here, drink this.

LILY: I knew something had happened.

FEATHER: What happened?

STAR: There were cannibals. Out on the lake.

HAIL: At this time of year?

FEATHER: What did they look like?

STAR: One used to be a Huron, the other a young Black Robe.

FEATHER: We should tell our Black Robe about him.

LILY: I think he already knows. Some sort of hunger was here
          tonight too.

HAIL: Is that what was wrong with him?

STAR: It was there, the great hunger. They were lost in it. I tried
          to make them turn around and go the other way. I
          thought I might be able to kill them both by myself.
          But they're still coming.

HAIL: This is the dream?

STAR: Part of it. We have to leave this place. There's a French-
          man with the men. He told us that the Iroquois are

on the warpath. They've burned the Huron villages down.

LILY: That's the other part.

HAIL: Where can we go?

STAR: The islands. With winter coming, the Iroquois won't be able to see us there.

FEATHER: I've never seen any Iroquois.

HAIL: You don't want to.

STAR: This is the dream.

LILY: The geese flying north in the fall. And eating each other instead of grass. Blood falls like sugar maple leaves onto the snow.

Scene Four

A foggy dawn. The sandy landing on the La Vase River shore below the village. The MOHAWK warrior enters, knife in hand, and moves along the water edge, reconnoitring. The blanket-cloaked Sky FEATHER enters. The MOHAWK hides in the rocks, watching her. She comes down to the shore to look out for the canoes, squats, disappointed, but looking down, notices his footprints. She looks for him, hesitates, starts to follow his tracks.

THISTLE: *(off)* Did you build up the fire? Girl? Girl, where are you? Answer me!

FEATHER: I'm here, mother!

THISTLE: *(off)* What are you doing out there?

FEATHER: I thought I heard the canoes, all right?

The MOHAWK slips further along the beach, exits.

THISTLE: *(off)* You heard the canoes?

THISTLE enters and comes down to the edge of the water beside Sky FEATHER.

THISTLE: I don't hear a thing.

FEATHER: Listen.

THISTLE: Staring at the water won't bring him back any quicker. You should leave that little 'old man' alone. He's too young for your love medicine.

FEATHER: I think he used love medicine on me.

THISTLE: Come back to the house.

FEATHER: No, mother, listen.

THISTLE: I want you to take the Father his banic. He'll be finished his prayers by now.

FEATHER: Listen. You hear?

THISTLE: Is that it?

FEATHER: That tap at the end of the stroke? Thunder Voice does that when he's tired.

THISTLE: Go tell Hail Stone Woman. Throw more meat in the pot. They'll be hungry.

FEATHER: Maybe they got a moose.

Two canoes enter out of the fog, Thunder VOICE and Fire CLOUD in the first with a load of moose meat and BEAR and IRON Man in the second with less meat and SAMUEL Argent.

THISTLE: I think they did. Husband! Son!

FEATHER: Is he there, mother?

CLOUD: Be quiet!

THISTLE: Of course he's there. Go on, you silly girl. Go on. Do as you're told.

FEATHER exits to the village.

THISTLE: Husband! Praise be to God! Husband!

CLOUD: Be quiet, woman!

THISTLE: What have you brought me? Is that moose meat?

CLOUD: Will you be quiet?

THISTLE: Is that another Black Robe for our church?

The canoes beach and the men disembark.

CLOUD: The Iroquois are on the warpath.

THISTLE: You're here now, husband. Why should I be afraid of the Iroquois? Our faith will protect us.

CLOUD: Listen to me—

THISTLE: You're not a Black Robe too?

Sky FEATHER and HAIL Stone Woman enter, come down to the water's edge.

CLOUD: Leave him alone, woman. The Iroquois are close by.

THISTLE: Father Noel has promised to save us.

IRON: The Iroquois killed all the Black Robes at Sainte Marie.

THISTLE: We need to be baptised.

HAIL: You went to Sainte Marie?

IRON: No, the Frenchman said so.

BEAR: They killed all the baptised Hurons there too.

HAIL: You were gone a long time.

IRON: We started travelling as soon as the rain let up.

CLOUD: And woman, your son killed an Iroquois last night.

THISTLE: You killed one last night?

CLOUD: We were camped by the dreamer's rock.

FEATHER: How's the little 'old man'?

BEAR: We thought it would be safe there.

FEATHER: Look at me.

THISTLE: Are you wounded?

FEATHER: You're not hurt?

CLOUD: He got grazed by a war club.

THISTLE: My little boy.

VOICE: I'm all right, woman.

THISTLE: I'm your mother!

FEATHER: You look tired.

VOICE: Here, sister. Come, take my bow.

THISTLE: You could have died! And you haven't been saved.

FATHER Noel enters.

HAIL: Your father came back last night.

BEAR: My father's here?

HAIL: Let him sleep. He was cold and tired.

BEAR exits to the village.

VOICE: What did he say this time?

HAIL: We're going to the islands. It will be safer there.

CLOUD: Be ready to go by midday.

HAIL: Come, husband, let's get those lazy daughters of yours
out of your bed.

HAIL Stone Woman and IRON Man exit.

VOICE: Sister, come help me get my canoe.

Thunder VOICE and Sky FEATHER exit along the shore.

FATHER: Martha, what's going on?

THISTLE: My husband says the Iroquois are close by.

FATHER: I knew it was true.

FATHER: Fire Cloud, you must all be baptised now.

CLOUD: What are you talking about?

FATHER: So if you're killed when the devils come, you'll have life
everlasting.

CLOUD: Out of my way, Black Robe.

THISTLE: I'll help Father Noel pack.

CLOUD: You and your daughter pack our own canoes first. Let the Frenchman help the Frenchman.

FATHER: Fire Cloud, wait.

CLOUD: Go pack your canoe if you're coming with us.

FATHER: You have to listen! Don't be stupid.

CLOUD: Where's my tobacco? *(he exits)*

THISTLE: No, Father, don't talk to him like that.

FATHER: Martha, my sister, if the Iroquois are so close, there's no time to waste.

THISTLE: I'll talk to him, Father. *(she exits)*

SAMUEL: Good day, Frenchman. You want some help?

FATHER: Who are you?

SAMUEL: Samuel Argent, Father.

FATHER: What are you?

SAMUEL: A trader in furs.

FATHER: Where did you come from?

SAMUEL: Sainte Marie.

FATHER: I don't know your name. Do you know Father Brébeuf?

SAMUEL: I saw him there.

FATHER: Are you a Christian?

SAMUEL: It depends. You got any communion wine left?

Sky FEATHER and Thunder VOICE enter, carrying a canoe.

FATHER: So you've lost yourself here in the wilderness. I've no time to help you find your way back.

SAMUEL: You don't want any help?

FATHER: These children need me more. *(he exits)*

SAMUEL Argent sees Sky FEATHER and Thunder VOICE and goes and takes the end of the canoe away from Sky FEATHER. BEAR enters as the young men carry the canoe down to the landing and Sky FEATHER goes to him.

FEATHER: Won't you speak to me?

VOICE: Sister, come away from him.

FEATHER: Don't be afraid of my brother. He's just a big noise.

VOICE: Come on. You know how his mother died.

THISTLE enters.

FEATHER: I don't care!

VOICE: Sister, come away. Don't talk to him.

THISTLE: Children, come with me!

BEAR: I can't have anything to do with you.

THISTLE: Father Noel will baptise you now!

BEAR: Someone's got to go to dreamer's rock this winter.

FEATHER: Why does it have to be you?

VOICE: Come on. Get away from him right now!

FEATHER: Let go of me! *(she runs away down the beach)*

VOICE: Sister!

FEATHER: Leave me alone! Leave me alone! *(she exits)*

THISTLE: Daughter? Where's she going?

VOICE: She was bothering the little 'old man'.

THISTLE: Let her go. She'll come back when she's hungry.

VOICE: But she shouldn't be out there now.

THISTLE: She's not as stupid as she acts. Come on. The Father's waiting for you.

Thunder VOICE and THISTLE exit toward the village.

BEAR: Samuel. Can the Black Robe's medicine save them from the Iroquois?

SAMUEL: It's not that kind of medicine.

BEAR: What good is it then?

SAMUEL: Bear, what did she mean?

BEAR: My father's awake now. He wants to talk to you.

SAMUEL: Your mother. How did she die?

BEAR: My father and I, we make medicine here. Another man was jealous of my father's power. His helpers killed my mother.

SAMUEL: His helpers? Who would kill a woman?

BEAR: My father won't say. Something that lives under the lake. That man, he took my mother's tongue for his medicine pouch.

SAMUEL: He took her tongue?

BEAR: My father has his tongue now.

SAMUEL: Can you and your father save us from the Iroquois?

BEAR: Come and talk with him.

Scene Five

The full moon rising. The forest. JOSEPH and PIERRE, much worse for wear, huddle together in a rock cleft.

PIERRE: I'm hungry, brother. Do you hear me? I'm hungry and cold. At least let me make a fire.

JOSEPH: The Iroquois will see where we are.

PIERRE: But there's going to be frost again tonight.

JOSEPH: Open your mouth. The moonlight is warm.

PIERRE: Brother, look at me.

JOSEPH: Warm as milk. And the dark is sweet. It's honey, brother, honey.

PIERRE: I can't eat the darkness of the night.

JOSEPH: This is the promised land, Pierre. Father Brébeuf will provide.

PIERRE: I'm hungry, Joseph.

JOSEPH: Loaves and fishes, dear Pierre, loaves and fishes.

PIERRE: I'm starving. Can't you get me another one of those little mice?

JOSEPH: Faith, Pierre, faith will deliver us. Our Father Who art in Heaven?

PIERRE: Our Father Who art in Heaven.

JOSEPH &
PIERRE: Hallowed be your name, may your kingdom come, may your will be done on Earth as it is in Heaven. Give us this day our daily—

PIERRE: (crying) Bread, bread, bread, daily bread, Joseph, daily bread—

JOSEPH: Quiet. Be quiet!

PIERRE: What is it?

JOSEPH: (unsheathing his knife) Someone's coming.

Sky FEATHER enters, stumbling through the dark. JOSEPH jumps Sky FEATHER. She screams, they struggle.

PIERRE: What are you doing? It's a woman. Joseph? Joseph!

JOSEPH pins Sky FEATHER down, covers her mouth.

JOSEPH: Loaves and fishes, Pierre!

The MOHAWK enters, knife in hand.

JOSEPH: Here's your little mouse!

The MOHAWK drags JOSEPH off Sky FEATHER, slits JOSEPH's throat. Sky FEATHER scrambles aside as JOSEPH falls, reaching out, dying.

PIERRE: *(stumbles forward)* Joseph? Joseph!

The MOHAWK threatens PIERRE. PIERRE exits in terror. Sky FEATHER scrambles to her feet, faces the MOHAWK. He puts his knife in its sheath.

VOICE: *(off, at a distance)* Sister!

The MOHAWK offers her a hand.

FEATHER: Brother! Brother, I'm here!

She starts to run but the MOHAWK tackles her, pins her down and forces a kiss on her, hands over her body. She struggles, bites him, he slaps her. She slaps him back. They look at each other.

VOICE: *(off, but nearer)* Sister? Sister, where are you?

Sky FEATHER kisses the MOHAWK, then grabs his hand, rubs it over her body. A long kiss, then she pulls him to his feet and leads him into an exit in a direction away from Thunder VOICE. JOSEPH's body glows in the moonlight.

Scene Six

The full moon high in the sky. The sandy landing on the La Vase River shore below the village. Four canoes almost packed and ready for departure lie at the edge of the sand. FLOOD Woman sits in IRON Man's canoe, rocking the restless baby boy North Star. HAIL Stone Woman and THISTLE stand nearby on the sand, HAIL Stone Woman with a paddle in her hand.

FLOOD: *(singing a lullaby)* Hush, now, hush, baby boy.
Go to sleep, deep as fish
Go to sleep. Hush, now, hush,
Stars close their eyes in the lake.

THISTLE: She'll be back soon.

HAIL: Black Star's making medicine to find her.

THISTLE: She'll be back. We don't need his help. Father Noel, he's praying for her.

HAIL: Well we can't wait. Not now.

THISTLE: I've been praying too.

HAIL: One of the men will find her.

THISTLE: I've been trying to pray. I should have made her talk to Father Noel. *(she begins to cry)*

HAIL: Someone will find her. We'll see you soon.

Baby boy North Star whines.

THISTLE: I'm going to go pray some more with the Father. *(she exits toward the village)*

HAIL: Quiet him. Someone's coming.

FLOOD: Hush, now, hush, baby boy...

CLOUD: *(entering along the beach)* Where's your husband, woman?

HAIL: Your wife's with the Black Robe.

CLOUD: What are you talking about?

HAIL: My husband's ready to go. We have to go now.

CLOUD: Has my daughter come back? We'll wait for her.

HAIL: No, we can't. My husband was down to the village at the point. He heard about Iroquois hunting down in the narrows into the bay.

IRON Man enters, carrying the crippled Star LILY.

CLOUD: We'll wait.

HAIL: We can't. Not with them that close.

IRON Man puts Star LILY down in the canoe beside FLOOD Woman.

CLOUD: This woman of yours, she says you want to leave.

IRON: The families at the point, they've already left. Their young men are singing their war songs. We'll go on ahead, prepare the hiding place.

CLOUD: What about my daughter?

HAIL: She's a stupid girl, chasing after that old man's son.

CLOUD: Can't you keep your woman quiet!

IRON: Get in the canoe. *(he takes the paddle from her)*

HAIL: Does he want us all to die on account of her? She's as good as dead by now

IRON: Get in! *(he slaps her butt with the paddle)*

HAIL Stone Woman gets in the canoe.

CLOUD: You're taking all that meat?

IRON: I have to look after my own women.

CLOUD: Wait till the others come back. Maybe one of them has found her.

LILY: Bear and the Frenchman came back already.

CLOUD: She wasn't in the east?

IRON: And you saw no sign north of here.

CLOUD: I found an Iroquois canoe. I tore the skin off it.

HAIL: They've got her for sure.

CLOUD: And Black Star?

LILY: He's singing. But he hasn't seen her.

FLOOD: Singing and singing.

LILY: He can't see her for the hunger.

FLOOD: Hush, now, hush, baby...

LILY: Winter's going to be bad.

HAIL: You're shivering.

LILY: The hunger's coming this way.

HAIL: Put the blanket on.

IRON: It'll be too light if we wait.

CLOUD: You're right.

IRON: We can't travel fast.

CLOUD: Go on then.

IRON Man pushes his canoe out into the lake.

HAIL: Husband, you know what they do to young women. Tell him I'm sorry.

           Clouds cover the moon.

IRON: My wife has a big mouth. She—

CLOUD: Go on!

           IRON Man jumps into his canoe with HAIL Stone Woman, FLOOD Woman and North Star. Fire CLOUD pushes it out of the shallows into an exit.

FLOOD: Hush, now, hush, baby boy. Go to sleep, deep as fish...

VOICE: *(off)* Father! Father!

CLOUD: Down here, boy. Here!

           Thunder VOICE enters, pushing PIERRE, arms bound behind his back, ahead of him.

VOICE: My sister's alive, father.

CLOUD: What? Where is she?

PIERRE: Please, I'm hungry and cold.

CLOUD: What's he saying? Does he know where she is?

VOICE: I think so, father. I heard my sister's voice. I heard her call me.

CLOUD: Where was this?

VOICE: The pines the other side of the swamp. But I couldn't find her.

CLOUD: It's all rocks over there.

VOICE: I couldn't find her trail.

Black STAR and BEAR enter.

PIERRE: Build me a fire tonight.

VOICE: But then I caught this one running out of the trees.

PIERRE: Please?

STAR: Put him down. Be careful. Are the thongs tight?

VOICE: I took him back into the rocks. There was a dead Huron there.

CLOUD: He kill him?

VOICE: I don't think so. He was afraid like a dog.

STAR: Did you burn the body? These are the cannibals I told you about.

VOICE: Are you sure?

STAR: A young Black Robe and a Huron.

CLOUD: He talks like the Black Robe.

VOICE: Does he know where she is?

PIERRE: A little mouse?

STAR: He's seen someone alive.

CLOUD: Look at the way he stares.

BEAR: Where's the body?

VOICE: The other side of the swamp.

STAR: Keep him tied tight.

VOICE: He doesn't look like a cannibal.

CLOUD: You've never seen one before.

Black STAR and BEAR exit.

CLOUD: Come on, you, on your feet.

VOICE: The Black Robe will make you tell us where she is.

Thunder VOICE pulls PIERRE to his feet and they exit, following Fire CLOUD.

Scene Seven

The full moon low in the sky. FATHER Noel kneels inside his wigwam in the middle of a prayer.

FATHER: Repel, O Lord, the power of the evil spirit! Dissolve the fallacies of its plots! May the unholy tempter take flight. May your servant be protected in soul and body by the sign of your name.

SAMUEL Argent enters, followed by THISTLE.

THISTLE: Why won't he speak to me? Make him speak to me.

SAMUEL picks up a load from beside the door.

FATHER: Preserve what is within this person. Rule his feelings. Strengthen his heart. Let the efforts of the enemy power be dispelled from his soul—

SAMUEL: He won't speak to me either.

THISTLE: Is he praying for my daughter?

SAMUEL: Except to give me orders.

THISTLE: Is that what he's doing? Praying for my daughter?

SAMUEL exits, carrying the load.

FATHER: By your most holy name. Grant the Grace that he who has inspired terror up to this time, now be put to flight and retire defeated—

THISTLE: Father! Father Noel! Do you know where my daughter is?

Fire CLOUD enters, followed by Thunder VOICE and the bound PIERRE.

CLOUD: Where is he? Where's the Black Robe?

THISTLE: Praying for our daughter.

SAMUEL Argent re-enters, still carrying his load. He puts it down.

FATHER: Let this man, your servant, be able to worship you with a firm heart and a sincere mind.

CLOUD: Black Robe, come out!

PIERRE: Loaves and fishes, loaves and fishes.

THISTLE: Who is this Frenchman, husband?

FATHER: Through Christ Our Lord. Amen.

CLOUD: Come out! Black Robe, come out here!

FATHER: *(coming out of the wigwam)* What do you want? Why are you disturbing the servant of the Lord at prayer?

CLOUD: We have brought you a young Black Robe.

FATHER: Untie him. Let him loose. Who are you?

PIERRE: I can't eat the darkness of the night.

VOICE: I found him in the woods. He knows where my sister is.

FATHER: Who are you? In the name of our Lord Jesus Christ, answer.

PIERRE: He is risen, he is risen!

CLOUD: Black Star said he came from Sainte Marie.

FATHER: Samuel Argent, come here. Do you know this man?

SAMUEL: No, Father.

FATHER: Untie him.

VOICE: Make him say where my sister is.

FATHER: Samuel!

SAMUEL: I don't think I should, Father.

FATHER: Why have you tied him up?

CLOUD: He's a cannibal.

THISTLE: Be careful, Father!

FATHER: That's madness. Let him go.

PIERRE: Father Brébeuf, he is risen!

FATHER: You know Father Brébeuf?

VOICE: Ask him about my sister. Ask him if he ate her.

THISTLE: Don't say that!

FATHER: This is a man of God.

VOICE: Ask him where my sister is!

FATHER: If he was at Sainte Marie, he has seen terrible things.

CLOUD: Has he seen my daughter?

FATHER: We must let him go. Martha, we must protect him. We are all the lambs of God.

THISTLE: Has he seen my daughter?

FATHER: He has seen terrible things.

THISTLE: Father, what about my daughter?

FATHER: Help me pray for him. Martha?

THISTLE kneels.

FATHER: John?

VOICE: Make him say where my sister is.

FATHER: I conjure you, ancient serpent, by the Judge of the living and the dead, by your maker, by the maker of the world, by him who has the power to cast you into everlasting fire, that from this servant of God, who hastens back to the bosom of the Church, you with the fears and afflictions of your fury speedily depart. Look at me. Look at me, brother!

PIERRE: Our Father Who art in Heaven?

FATHER: Have you seen their daughter? In the woods.

PIERRE: A little mouse, yes.

FATHER: In the name of our Lord Jesus Christ, answer.

PIERRE: The woman, yes. An Iroquois warrior was there. He took her.

FATHER: An Iroquois warrior was there.

CLOUD: He'll try to take her away.

THISTLE: My baby girl.

FATHER: He took her.

CLOUD: We'll go to that canoe.

THISTLE: Save my baby girl!

CLOUD: Wife, stay with the Black Robes. Go wait on the beach.

Fire CLOUD and Thunder VOICE exit.

FATHER: Thank you, my son. What's your name? *(he unties the thongs)*

PIERRE: I'm Pierre, Father.

FATHER: The foundation of our faith.

PIERRE: I'm hungry and cold, Father.

FATHER: Martha! Martha, get him something to eat.

THISTLE: Father, bring him to the canoes. We got to be ready to leave...

FATHER: Have faith, Martha. Our Lord will preserve your daughter.

THISTLE: I believe you, Father.

FATHER: This is Pierre, Martha. He too is a lamb of God.

PIERRE: Father Brébeuf is walking on the water.

THISTLE: Come with me. Come on. I'll get you something to eat.

THISTLE and PIERRE exit toward the beach.

FATHER: You have work to do.

SAMUEL: *(picking the load back up)* Yes, Father. *(he exits)*

FATHER Noel goes into his wigwam and kneels down before the altar.

FATHER: Glory be to the Father, and to the Son, and to the Holy Spirit. As it was in beginning, is now and shall be, for ever and ever.

Scene Eight

The full moon is setting. The sandy landing on the La Vase River shore below the village. The three canoes packed and ready for departure lie at the edge of the sand. PIERRE sits in the middle of FATHER Noel's canoe, nibbling on a piece of banic. THISTLE stands beside the canoe. FATHER Noel kneels nearby on the sand, praying silently. PIERRE raps against the side of the canoe and THISTLE hands him another piece.

THISTLE: You poor thing.

PIERRE: I'm hungry and cold. Build me a fire.

THISTLE: What's he say, Father? Father Noel?

FATHER: He's thanking God for you, Martha.

PIERRE: A fire tonight.

THISTLE: Father, why is he so strange?

SAMUEL Argent enters from the village.

FATHER: He was at Sainte Marie.

THISTLE: But he's not wounded.

FATHER: His spirit is.

A glow begins in the sky to the south.

THISTLE: Black Star says he's a cannibal.

FATHER: Christians don't believe in cannibals.

SAMUEL: They've never met the Iroquois. No sign along the path.

PIERRE: *(standing up, pointing)* Fire, fire, fire, fire!

THISTLE: What's wrong with him?

SAMUEL: Look. That glow.

THISTLE: Something's on fire.

SAMUEL: That's the village by the point.

PIERRE: Fire and smoke rising up to heaven.

SAMUEL: That must be where the Iroquois are.

FATHER: Don't cry, Martha.

THISTLE: I'm not crying.

FATHER: Have faith.

THISTLE: Pierre's crying.

SAMUEL: I think we should go.

THISTLE: We can't leave!

SAMUEL: Father, we can't travel as fast as the rest of them.

FATHER: I will not abandon my flock.

PIERRE raps for more banic.

SAMUEL: And with that one along? You know how Iroquois hate the sight of you.

THISTLE: Our faith will protect us.

SAMUEL: It's not our spirits I'm worried about.

THISTLE: Father, isn't that so?

SAMUEL: What do you think they'll do to the Father and his little brother there if they catch them?

PIERRE: Father Brébeuf is walking on the water!

FATHER: Sit down, Pierre. Sit!

SAMUEL: Think what they've already done to him.

THISTLE: Father, maybe you should go on ahead.

FATHER: I don't want to leave you.

THISTLE: Make sure poor Pierre gets away.

FATHER: But we don't know where to go.

SAMUEL: You come with us. Show us the way.

THISTLE: But my daughter—

SAMUEL: Staying here won't do her any good. And you can pray for her soul just well on the water. Am I right, Father? Isn't that what a Christian woman would do?

THISTLE: But there's not enough room in the Father's canoe.

The moon is down.

SAMUEL: It'll be light soon.

PIERRE: I'm hungry. I'm hungry!

SAMUEL: The three of you go. You know I can hide if I have to.

THISTLE: Come on, Father. *(she gets into the canoe)*

FATHER: Are you sure?

PIERRE raps the canoe. FATHER Noel gets into the canoe and picks up his paddle.

FATHER: Bless you, Samuel Argent.

SAMUEL: Get going.

PIERRE: Make me a fire tonight?

SAMUEL: Go on before I make you change places with me.

SAMUEL Argent shoves the canoe out of the shallows.

PIERRE: Make me a fire? *(he waves goodbye)*

SAMUEL Argent waves goodbye as FATHER Noel, PIERRE and THISTLE, in the canoe, exit. SAMUEL squats down, his head in his hands. BEAR enters from down the beach.

BEAR: The Black Robes, where are they?

SAMUEL: I sent them and the Christian woman on ahead.

BEAR: Good. Women and men in skirts are slow.

SAMUEL: What are you smiling about?

BEAR: We got him! The Mohawk who raped Sky Feather. All four of us. Talk about stupid. *(he pushes Black STAR's canoe out into the shallows)*

SAMUEL: You went to burn the cannibal.

BEAR: We did. That Huron went up like tinder. But then my father picked up the Mohawk's trail. We came up behind him and Fire Cloud and Thunder Voice were already there waiting.

The glow in the sky turns blood red as the dawn comes up.

SAMUEL: At his canoe?

SAMUEL Argent helps BEAR push Fire CLOUD's canoe into the shallows.

BEAR: He had his hands all over her. Didn't notice the canoe was wrecked. And didn't see us till it was too late.

Fire CLOUD enters, his arm around Sky FEATHER, leading her toward the canoes.

BEAR: Thunder Voice had his war club ready. It sounded like an axe going into walnut wood.

SAMUEL: She crying?

BEAR: Ya. Hasn't said a word. Come on, steady it for them.

SAMUEL Argent and BEAR hold the canoe for Fire CLOUD and Sky FEATHER. Thunder VOICE, Black STAR and the MOHAWK enter. The MOHAWK's arms are bound and he's gagged. He's bloody and bruised. Thunder VOICE has a hold on the rope and he jerks it, making the MOHAWK stumble.

VOICE: Get up, Iroquois. Come on, you're going for a ride.

Thunder VOICE drags the MOHAWK along on the sand and into the water.

SAMUEL: We're taking him with us?

BEAR: He has to pay for what he did.

STAR: Hold it steady.

Thunder VOICE gets in the canoe and tugs the MOHAWK up close to the hull.

SAMUEL: He'll drown.

STAR: Thunder Voice won't let that won't happen.

VOICE: It would spoil the fun.

BEAR and Black STAR push the canoe off.

SAMUEL: What's going to happen to him?

STAR: A warrior's death.

VOICE: It's better than he deserves.

Thunder VOICE and Fire CLOUD paddle their canoe off, towing the MOHAWK beside them. Black STAR and BEAR step into their canoe.

STAR: It's getting light.

BEAR: Come on. Come on, the Iroquois will see us.

SAMUEL Argent pushes the canoe off and hops in between them. They start paddling off through the bloody dawn.

Scene Nine

Dusk. The new village on Great Manitou Island in Lake Nipissing. In a wig-wam away from the others THISTLE embraces Sky FEATHER. Intermittent drumming, singing, shouting come from the dance ground.

THISTLE: Come on now. Come on. Enough of this. You got to come to the dance ground tonight.

FEATHER: I can't do it.

THISTLE: Your father says you have to come.

FEATHER: Tell him I'll do it tomorrow night.

THISTLE: This is your last chance. The Mohawk is strong but he'll die soon. He'll die tonight.

FEATHER: I don't want to look at him.

THISTLE: You're clean now. You're strong. You've had the medicines, the songs. Star Lily made that song just for you.

FEATHER: I don't want to see him again.

THISTLE: Flood Woman will come get you when it's time.

FEATHER: Mother, wait. I looked into his eyes.

THISTLE: You'll look into them again. Make him see what he gets for doing this to one of our women. You must caress him with flame.

FEATHER: I looked into his eyes. Mother, he's only a man.

THISTLE: They're all only men.

FEATHER: You told me the Iroquois were evil spirits.

THISTLE: He'll be a spirit soon enough. He's got to go into the next world with the warning branded in his skin.

FEATHER: He has to die?

THISTLE: He's Iroquois.

FEATHER: Mother, he didn't force me. When I looked into his eyes, when I saw who he was, I decided to go with him.

THISTLE: He's Iroquois. They're known for their love medicines.

FEATHER: He didn't hurt me.

THISTLE: He was beautiful. But your father and your brother and Iron Man, they're dancing for you now. You've got to show them how strong you are.

FEATHER: Dancing so they'll be brave to raid the Iroquois.

THISTLE: Of course they'll be brave. The Iroquois are burning all our people's villages.

FATHER Noel and Star LILY, using a crutch, enter.

THISTLE: The women there, they're losing their noses, their hair. Listen to me. They're losing their babies.

LILY: Stay here, Black Robe.

FATHER: Is that where she is?

LILY: Stay here!

THISTLE: Your father's oldest sister? One of your cousin's came over with the news. She's gone on to the next world.

LILY: That's a woman's house.

THISTLE: We may never be able to bury her bones.

LILY: Even a man in a skirt might get hurt.

PIERRE enters.

FATHER: Say I want her to pray with me.

LILY: I'll get her for you. Just stay put.

FEATHER: I don't want him to look at me.

Star LILY raps on the door post.

LILY: The Black Robe's here.

FATHER: Martha! Martha, will you talk to me now?

THISTLE: *(coming out)* I told you before. Don't call me that any-more.

FATHER: Martha, I need you to help me.

THISTLE: My husband told me to stay away from you now.

FATHER: You're my sister. Please.

Star LILY enters the wigwam.

THISTLE: He says your god's no good.

FATHER: They have to stop hurting that poor man.

THISTLE: That man's Iroquois.

FATHER: They have to pray for forgiveness. You shall not kill. We are God's lambs, Martha. You shall not kill. Black Star and Bear must stop singing their witchcraft songs.

PIERRE: I'm hungry and cold.

THISTLE: Why did your god let that Iroquois hurt my daughter?

FATHER: Martha, they force him to eat his own filth.

LILY: You have to kill the Iroquois.

FEATHER: Go away.

FATHER: They pulled the nails off all his fingers and toes. They burned the bloody stumps!

THISTLE: Go back to your house, Father.

PIERRE: Give us this day our bread?

THISTLE: This is none of your business.

FATHER: You won't eat his heart, will you? Are you devils yourselves?

THISTLE: My husband said you'd be weaker than any woman.

LILY: Put an end to his misery.

FEATHER: Why should I?

LILY: A knife in his heart will do it.

FATHER: It's horrible. Horrible.

The waning moon starts to rise.

LILY: Then you can tell your son his father died without tears, a warrior's death.

FEATHER: My son?

LILY: Your baby. Do you want the Black Robe to get his hands on it? *(she leaves the wigwam)*

PIERRE: Our daily bread?

FATHER: I saw Hail Stone Woman take a burning stick.

THISTLE: Go take care of little Pierre.

FATHER: She poked him in ways that aren't decent.

PIERRE: I'm hungry.

THISTLE: Keep him away from us, Father.

FATHER: Thunder Voice pulled the man's thumb off!

THISTLE: If he turns into a cannibal, my husband will have to kill him.

THISTLE enters the wigwam and Sky FEATHER embraces her.

FATHER: The man's thumb! He's going around teasing Flood Woman with it.

LILY: I think he wants her to marry him.

PIERRE: Another little mouse?

LILY: Come along.

FATHER: I think the Iroquois will die tonight.

LILY: I think you're right, Black Robe.

FATHER: Pierre? Pierre will help me give him the last rites at least.

LILY: Come away from here.

FATHER: And a Christian burial.

LILY: You're going back to your house.

FATHER: Pierre, come along!

Star LILY leads FATHER Noel off.

PIERRE: Please. I'm cold.

FEATHER: Mother... I'll come tonight.

THISTLE: You will?

FEATHER: I'll look into his eyes.

PIERRE: Build me a fire?

FEATHER: I'll caress him with steel.

THISTLE: I'll go tell your father.

FEATHER: Let's go now. I'm hungry.

PIERRE: I'm hungry and cold.

FEATHER: I want to look at him for a while first.

PIERRE: A fire tonight? Please? Please!

THISTLE and Sky FEATHER leave the wigwam and exit. PIERRE follows them off.

END OF ACT ONE

ACT TWO

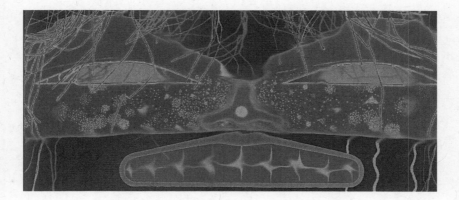

Scene One

A dawn clear after a late winter storm on Great Manitou Island. SAMUEL Argent is in the forest, digging for fire wood in the snow, a bundle of sticks nearby. PIERRE enters, snowshoeing across the surface, carrying a small cross made of sticks over his shoulder.

PIERRE: Who's there?

SAMUEL: Greetings, Pierre.

PIERRE: Is that you, brother? Bless me.

SAMUEL: What have you got there?

PIERRE: Bless me, for I have sinned.

SAMUEL: Can I look?

PIERRE: No!

SAMUEL: I could use that. Come on, little Father. Give it here.

PIERRE: No.

SAMUEL: What have you been up to?

PIERRE: He is risen, brother!

SAMUEL: You reek of death.

PIERRE: Fire and smoke! Rising up to heaven!

SAMUEL: Get away from me! Get off!

PIERRE: He is risen!

SAMUEL: Go on!

FATHER: *(off)* Pierre! Pierre, wait for me!

PIERRE: Oh no! Noise noise noise!

SAMUEL: I hear you, brother.

FATHER: *(off)* Pierre?

PIERRE: It's those damned flies! Damn flies! *(he exits at a run)*

SAMUEL Argent goes back to work. FATHER Noel enters.

FATHER: Samuel? Is that you? Samuel! Won't you speak? I didn't recognize you.

SAMUEL: He went that way.

FATHER: You look thin.

SAMUEL: Better go after him.

FATHER: You don't get enough food.

SAMUEL: He shouldn't be wandering around loose.

FATHER: You must come and stay with us now.

SAMUEL: If Black Star catches Pierre he'll give him the cure.

FATHER: Is that mountebank back?

SAMUEL: He'll put him out of his misery.

FATHER: He has no right to do that! You shall not kill.

SAMUEL: Nobody's back.

FATHER: That servant of the devil!

SAMUEL: They think Pierre's a devil.

FATHER: If he dares touch that poor creature—

SAMUEL: It might make him a man again.

FATHER: He will answer to the Lord God on high.

SAMUEL: You're right, Father.

FATHER: It's superstition.

SAMUEL: He's getting away on you.

FATHER: You know that. You were born into the true faith. You know Pierre was sent to test us in these last days.

SAMUEL: 'Only prayer will heal his soul.' What do you want, Father? I'm tired.

FATHER: You're hungry. It would be best for you to be with your own kind.

SAMUEL: You and Pierre?

FATHER: These are the last days and you're all alone.

SAMUEL: They'll be back.

FATHER: It's too late, Samuel.

SAMUEL: I've got work to do. I'll freeze if my fire goes out.

FATHER: Do you know what today is?

SAMUEL: Don't trouble yourself about me, Father.

FATHER: Your fire doesn't matter now.

SAMUEL: Remember, Father. You told me yourself. I'm one of the lost.

FATHER: This is Holy Friday. The fires of hell are coming.

SAMUEL: Maybe the fires of the Iroquois.

FATHER: I've come to invite you to celebrate with us, my son. To be with us when the end comes.

SAMUEL: So what have you got to eat?

FATHER: Do you repent your sin?

SAMUEL: Black Star tells me I might make a good singer.

FATHER: No, Samuel, that's heathenish. When did you last take communion?

SAMUEL: At Sainte Marie.

FATHER: You must come and be with us. Don't let them lead you astray. That boy, his father, they're charlatans.

SAMUEL: I like them.

FATHER: They're the children of the devil.

SAMUEL: And you and Pierre are the children of God?

FATHER: I know I have failed in my mission here. There are still witches among them.

SAMUEL: Witches? What are you talking about?

FATHER: That girl, that cripple.

SAMUEL: She's fasting, Father. Don't Christians fast? Star Lily's fasting.

FATHER: I've lost John. Only Martha has been saved.

SAMUEL: She's getting in touch with the spirits. It's like prayer.

FATHER: Only Martha.

SAMUEL: Everybody else is scared of you. Black Star told them you scared the game away.

FATHER: What do you mean?

SAMUEL: You brought all the bad weather. You caused the famine.

FATHER: How can they believe that?

SAMUEL: Father, Black Robes were the ones who brought them small pox.

FATHER: That man is the devil.

SAMUEL: He's just trying to protect his family.

FATHER: All of those lost here in the wilderness will answer for their sins. All of those who repent will be forgiven their weaknesses. He will forgive you your weakness with that boy.

SAMUEL: Father Noel, look at me. I'm not lost. I belong here.

FATHER: No, you will come to our celebration.

SAMUEL: Go to hell.

FATHER: But this is hell, my son. This is hell. Soon He will raise us up to heaven. As He rose on the third day, so shall we all rise up to heaven.

SAMUEL: Is that why Pierre's running around in the woods carrying a cross like the Saviour himself?

FATHER: He has a cross?

SAMUEL: 'Bless me, for I have sinned!'

FATHER: Even Pierre knows the time is close!

SAMUEL: Go after him, Father.

FATHER: The end of the world is at hand.

SAMUEL: He might get hurt.

FATHER: Please come, Samuel. He provides for his children. It's like Pierre says. Loaves and fishes. You must come and take the last supper with us.

SAMUEL turns, picks up his bundle and exits.

FATHER: *(kneeling in the snow)* I'll pray for your salvation.

Scene Two

The same clear morning. A winter hunting camp on the north shore of Lake Nipissing. Fire CLOUD's drinking tea, Thunder VOICE and IRON Man are drowsing.

CLOUD: *(rising to his feet)* Someone's coming.

BEAR enters from the woods on snowshoes.

CLOUD: Where were you?

BEAR: We had to dig in when the storm hit. Is that hot?

CLOUD: Here.

IRON: I almost got lost too.

CLOUD: I thought it might just blow over.

BEAR: No, my father had to fight it.

IRON: Four days of wind.

VOICE: He's always fighting the weather. What about the Iroquois?

CLOUD: Show respect. The Iroquois are asleep in their fort.

IRON: Dreaming up nightmares for us.

CLOUD: Where's your father?

BEAR: He made me some medicine, then took his drum and disappeared into the storm.

CLOUD: We should look for him.

BEAR: No. The storm's retreated. He'll be back.

VOICE: The old man's lost.

CLOUD: We'll help you.

BEAR: No. The rest of you should go home. Cross the ice now.

VOICE: My father will decide what to do.

BEAR: I'll wait here for my father. We'll be all right.

IRON: We've nothing to show the women.

VOICE: We can't go now.

BEAR: It's a cannibal spirit, a hunger greater than any he ever met before.

VOICE: Maybe he's just getting old and small.

BEAR: I'm too tired to play with you and your big noise. This is what my father said.

VOICE: You can't scare me.

BEAR: Oh, are you a Christian again? Hiding behind the white man's skirt?

VOICE: There's no place you can hide from me.

CLOUD: There's no time for this. Behave yourselves.

VOICE: They never bring us anything to eat! What good are they?

CLOUD: Stop it. I'm sure his father's right. I've never seen a blizzard like it before myself. It was like the northern lights were angry.

IRON: I heard the ice shifting.

VOICE: That's stupid. It's too cold.

BEAR: My father, he's worried about the women. *(he lies down in the shelter)*

IRON: Could the hunger be that big?

VOICE: It will be spring soon. The Iroquois are more dangerous than any ice demon.

BEAR: He thinks someone with the Iroquois is feeding it.

VOICE: No one would do that!

CLOUD: We should cross now.

IRON: Who knows when it will be as easy to travel?

VOICE: You're talking like old women.

IRON: His father's worried about the women. Think about my daughter, your wife.

VOICE: The little 'old man' is staying behind?

BEAR: Will you miss me?

VOICE: I'm halfway home already.

CLOUD: Then get moving.

IRON: It's good for you you're too small for Black Star to see.

CLOUD: What do you need?

BEAR: That dried fish is enough. I saw new tracks on the way here.

IRON: Maybe we'll find something on the way home too.

Thunder VOICE, Fire CLOUD and IRON Man exit. BEAR closes his eyes.

Scene Three

Late the same day, a green dusk settles into the forest on Great Manitou Island. THISTLE is gathering wood. Sky FEATHER, six months pregnant, enters.

FEATHER: Mother!

THISTLE: What are you doing outside?

FEATHER: I really had to pee, all right?

THISTLE: You should be watching the fire.

FEATHER: There's plenty of wood. The fire won't starve.

THISTLE: You shouldn't be walking around.

FEATHER: You were going for food?

THISTLE: All these branches came down in the storm.

FEATHER: There's plenty of wood. We can't eat wood, mother. We're not beaver. Here. I'll take care of it.

THISTLE: Careful.

FEATHER: I'm not sick.

THISTLE: You are strong. I got weak carrying your brother.

FEATHER: He's a big load. You said Hail Stone Woman might have something left.

THISTLE: She had all those pumpkins.

FEATHER: You want me to go ask her?

THISTLE: We gave her that corn. You like pumpkin soup.

FEATHER: Pumpkin would do.

THISTLE: Think about Star Lily.

FEATHER: Does she have something to eat?

THISTLE: Do you hear her complaining?

FEATHER: How could I? You won't let me near the women's house.

THISTLE: Don't be stupid.

FEATHER: She shouldn't have to sing. She's a little girl.

THISTLE: She's growing up fast. She knows what she's doing. Didn't she know about my grandchild? Fasting isn't that hard.

FEATHER: When there's nothing to eat.

THISTLE: You young women should only fast in the spring.

FEATHER: She wouldn't need to fast if Black Star was here.

THISTLE: There won't be berries to break her fast with.

FEATHER: It's too long since she started.

THISTLE: Since the new moon. It'll be full soon. Her helpers will come to her by then. Here. Tie up the bundle.

FEATHER: She'll see where the birds are.

THISTLE: —why there are no fish under the ice. I think it's because the men are on the warpath in winter. Don't the Iroquois feel the cold? It used to be so peaceful in winter. We used to tell stories.

FEATHER: They want all the beaver skins.

THISTLE: They should talk to the beaver and leave us alone. If they stayed inside, they wouldn't get cold. Why do they want beaver skins with us hungry?

FEATHER: They don't know we're here, mother.

THISTLE: I'll pray for them to die.

FEATHER: Black Robe medicine won't help.

PIERRE enters, still carrying the stick-cross.

THISTLE: It can't hurt. He says the English are devils.

PIERRE: Who's there?

THISTLE: It's us, little Father.

FEATHER: I'm cold.

PIERRE: Bless me? Bless me?

FEATHER: I'm going back to the house.

THISTLE: Take the bundle with you. I'll go see about that pumpkin.

FEATHER: Be careful of him. *(she exits the way she came)*

PIERRE: Bless me, for I have sinned.

THISTLE: What have you got? I made that. Give it here.

PIERRE: No. No!

THISTLE: Why have you got that? Father will be angry with you.

PIERRE: I'm hungry and cold.

THISTLE: You poor thing. You don't know any better.

PIERRE: Make me a fire tonight?

THISTLE: Do you want some banic? Me too. Here now.

THISTLE takes the cross away from PIERRE.

PIERRE: No! I'm hungry.

THISTLE: You got to learn to share.

PIERRE: I'm hungry and cold!

THISTLE: This belongs to the Iroquois. *(she finishes tying up her second bundle of sticks)*

PIERRE: Bless me! Bless me!

THISTLE: We're going to put it back. Come on. Let's go. Are you coming? What will I tell Father Noel? Come on. *(she exits)*

PIERRE starts to follow her off, then hesitates.

THISTLE: *(off)* Come on!

PIERRE exits, following her.

Scene Four

BEAR is still waiting by the fire at the winter hunting camp that still starry night when Black STAR stumbles out of the dark woods, with only his drum and bow and an oak branch for support through the snow and his fatigue.

BEAR: Father? What happened?

Black STAR gestures for silence. BEAR jumps up and guides him to the fire, gets him some tea. Black STAR drinks and catches his breath.

STAR: In my pouch.

BEAR: Meat! Porcupine? My mouth's watering.

STAR: Put it in the pot. The others?

BEAR: Left this morning.

STAR: They should be across the ice by now. I'm going to rest.

BEAR: Was it the Iroquois?

STAR: Till the fire burns down. *(he lies down)*

BEAR: Father?

STAR: No. But they've come out of their fort.

BEAR: We'll go home in the morning?

STAR: No. As soon as we eat.

BEAR: Are they that close?

STAR: I could see their fires from the top of the hill. Wake me when the meat's ready.

BEAR: What happened? Tell me. The wind blew right in under the blanket. The ashes rose up around the fire. You said that something was coming toward us. You said to stay awake.

STAR: I had to go out to meet it.

BEAR: Was it the cannibal spirit?

STAR: I walked a long way through the wind, the snow.

BEAR: You lost your snowshoes.

The northern lights appear.

STAR: I sang, talked a lot to my helpers. I came to a place, a lot of little bushes.

BEAR: But this branch is from a full grown oak.

STAR: Listen to me. The wind blew around and around me there, but I just sang louder.

BEAR: I bet you were as loud as the cannibal was.

STAR: I felt as big as the blizzard. My helpers were with me. That's when they told me.

BEAR: What is it?

STAR: One of our own people. From the village at the point. He's helping the Iroquois make this medicine.

BEAR: A Christian?

STAR: Someone hungry for fur. Someone who wants many guns for himself.

BEAR: How would he carry them all?

STAR: The cannibal's strong. I almost broke in half. It got away.

BEAR: It got away?

STAR: I didn't kill it. It's hungry. It seemed to have many bodies. It'll be back.

BEAR: We have to warn the others.

STAR: When I woke up, it was gone. I was sitting there in the snow, no clothes on, only that stick in my hand protecting me.

BEAR: No frost bite? Bet it got really small in the cold. Will it fall off?

STAR: Show respect. I'm your father.

BEAR: Have some more tea.

STAR: It was really small.

BEAR: You're dressed now.

STAR: My clothes and bow were along the trail.

BEAR: Did it eat all your arrows?

STAR: I had one left. And that porcupine was just sitting up there in a tree in the sun. I thanked my helpers then.

BEAR: You should go to sleep.

STAR: The wind was down. It seemed warm. The snow was all trampled and the little oaks all broken.

BEAR: I can hear the wind now.

STAR: But I can't remember how it all happened.

BEAR: Coming across the lake.

STAR: That smells good. *(he closes his eyes)*

BEAR: I'll wake you up when it's done.

STAR: Then we'll go across to my dreaming rock.

The northern lights watch over them.

Scene Five

The same starry night. HAIL Stone Woman's inside her wigwam, half asleep, with FLOOD Woman, tending the fire, and the restless baby boy North Star.

HAIL: Make him be quiet! Don't look at me like that. Feed him.

FLOOD: He hates that tea. It doesn't stop his hunger.

HAIL: Give him to me.

FLOOD: Why?

HAIL: I have to try. *(she picks North Star up to nurse him)*
            Hush, now, hush, baby boy.
            Go to sleep, deep as fish
            Go to sleep. Hush, now, hush...

FLOOD: I had a dream.

Clouds begin blanketing the stars.

HAIL: Where's the tea?

FLOOD: The men came back with a moose.

HAIL: There's no tea. The water's all gone.

FLOOD: I'm sorry. I forgot. I'll go now. *(she wraps herself up in a
            blanket, picks up the pail)*

HAIL: You have the axe?

FLOOD: I left it there.

HAIL: Someone could take it. Do you know how many beaver
            skins that cost your father?

FLOOD: Who would take it?

HAIL: The Black Robe takes things. Make sure you bring the
            axe back this time.

FLOOD: All right. *(she leaves the wigwam and exits)*

HAIL: Moose! Silly girl. Rabbit would do. North Star will
            dream about rabbit now, won't you? No, don't cry.
            Close your eyes and dream me a rabbit. That's it. You're

a good boy. Your father will come soon with his kill. Thunder Voice will bring you food to eat too. Yes, he will. He's your sister's husband now and he wants your sister to give him a son. A man who can't feed his wife should hide his face.

FLOOD: *(off)* Mother!

HAIL: No, no, don't wake up. *(she lies North Star down)*

FLOOD: *(off)* Mother, look what I've got!

HAIL: *(coming out of the wigwam)* Not so loud.

FLOOD: *(enters, carrying the better part of a large, frozen, and peculiar-looking sturgeon)* But, Mother, look! Look at this! I've got a fish!

HAIL: Where did you get that?

FLOOD: I've got a fish!

HAIL: There's enough here for the rest of the winter!

FLOOD: When I chopped through the ice, it just floated up in the hole.

HAIL: It just floated up?

FLOOD: In the water hole!

HAIL: It's frozen solid.

FLOOD: Chop off a piece.

HAIL: So where's the axe?

FLOOD: I was so excited—

HAIL: Well go get it.

FLOOD: Oh Momma, I've been so hungry.

HAIL: Well we're going to eat now.

FLOOD: I was so tired of corn broth.

HAIL: I couldn't tell by the way it went down

FLOOD: I was afraid I was turning into an Iroquois.

HAIL: Go get the axe.

           The night is black.

FLOOD: I'm going. *(she exits)*

HAIL: *(taking the fish into the wigwam)* This should be fine. As
           soon as you thaw.

           The fish starts to glow.

HAIL   There's nothing wrong with you, is there? The way you
           stare. All this ice. You're so beautiful.

FLOOD: *(entering)* Here it is.

HAIL: *(blocking the doorway)* And the water?

FLOOD: I'm so hungry, I can't think straight.

HAIL: I want to let it swim in soup. Give it here.

FLOOD: I'll be right back. *(she exits)*

HAIL: *(moves to chop the fish up but stops)* Don't look at me that
           way. I have to. Isn't this why you came? Who would
           send you? Covered in frost. How do you know my
           name?

FLOOD: *(entering)* Here's the water.

HAIL: *(blocking the doorway)* I'll put it in the pot.

FLOOD: All right. You want me to chop it up?

HAIL: I want you to go over, tell Thistle she and Sky Feather are invited.

FLOOD: But this is our fish.

HAIL: She gave us what she could before. It's our turn now.

FLOOD: All she gave us was the corn.

HAIL: No. It'll take time to thaw. Now go.

FLOOD: Should I go by the women's house too?

HAIL: The women's house?

FLOOD: My sister can break her fast.

HAIL: If you like.

FLOOD: I'll be right back. *(she exits)*

North Star whines.

HAIL: All right. Now what? No. Nobody here would throw your bones in the lake. Maybe the Black Robe. Are you looking for him? Are you the blizzard? *(she lifts the sturgeon to her lips)* It's too late now. I'm so sleepy. *(she takes a bite, chews and swallows)* You're so beautiful. *(she takes another bite)*

North Star starts to cry. HAIL Stone Woman is suddenly shaken by cramps, drops the fish, falls down in the snow.

HAIL: Flood Woman. Flood Woman! Daughter! *(she writhes, screams in pain)*

North Star cries. The sturgeon glows with a spectral light.

Scene Six

The same black night, FATHER Noel, in his wigwam in the forest, is kneeling down by the fire, praying.

FATHER: To you do we cry, poor banished children of Eve. To you do we send up our sighs, mourning and weeping in this valley of tears. Turn, then, most gracious mother, your merciful eyes toward us. And, after this our exile, show us—

PIERRE enters, driven forward by MARTHA waving the stick-cross.

THISTLE: Go on!

PIERRE: Please, I'm hungry.

THISTLE: Get in there! Father! Father Noel?

FATHER: Who's there?

THISTLE: Father, it's me!

FATHER: Martha?

THISTLE: Father, I've brought you Pierre.

THISTLE pushes PIERRE in through the door flap and follows him.

FATHER: Martha, I prayed for you to come.

PIERRE: I'm hungry and—Fire!

THISTLE: Sit down. Sit.

FATHER: Welcome.

THISTLE: Father, do you know what he's done?

FATHER: Sit down, Martha, please sit down. I sent him out to find you. And he has!

PIERRE: Fire and smoke.

THISTLE: Are you crying, Father? What's wrong?

FATHER: The end of the world has come. I didn't want to be alone.

PIERRE: Rising up to heaven. To heaven!

THISTLE: Be quiet!

FATHER: Poor man. Whatever he did cannot matter now. We're together now. All of us.

THISTLE: Father Noel, look at this.

FATHER: The most holy cross our Lord died on this day over sixteen centuries ago.

THISTLE: Father, it's the cross I made for the Iroquois' grave.

FATHER: Give it to me. Is it not beautiful?

PIERRE: I'm cold.

FATHER: Don't you love it?

PIERRE: Hungry and cold.

FATHER: We will celebrate the last supper together here before it in the wilderness. All our sins will be forgiven.

THISTLE: Father, I think he's been eating the Iroquois' body.

FATHER: We will celebrate together and prepare for his coming.

THISTLE: Father, listen to me.

FATHER: Yes, I can hear him coming now!

THISTLE: The body's lying there in the snow. It's all pulled apart!

PIERRE: Give us this day our daily bread?

THISTLE: Father Noel, look at me!

FATHER: Sit down, Martha, please.

THISTLE: Birds had been trying to eat the eyes but they're frozen.

FATHER: He'll be here any moment.

THISTLE: Pierre's a cannibal, Father Noel.

FATHER: He's coming to feed his children.

THISTLE: He's your brother. It's up to you to kill him now before he gets strong. Kill him or he'll eat the rest of us.

FATHER: Do you know what he'll say to us? He'll say Take and eat this.

THISTLE: Let go of me, Father Noel.

FATHER: He'll say, This is my body, my warm body.

PIERRE: Forgive us our trespasses.

THISTLE: Let go! You're hurting me.

FATHER: He'll say, Drink this.

THISTLE: You cut me!

FATHER: Drink. This is my blood.

THISTLE: I'm bleeding.

FATHER Noel touches THISTLE's cut and then licks the blood from his fingers.

PIERRE: Loaves? Loaves and fishes.

THISTLE: What's the matter with you? Stop it!

FATHER: My warm blood. Those who are thirsty—

THISTLE breaks and scurries away from FATHER Noel, out of the wigwam.

FATHER: Martha? Sister, where are you going?

THISTLE: Don't you call me that!

PIERRE: I'm cold now.

THISTLE: You're the one!

PIERRE: Why am I cold?

THISTLE: It was you all along! *(she exits in terror off into the night)*

FATHER: She's gone, Pierre, she's gone. Gone to hell. I've failed again. A witch will not be—

The unearthly howl. PIERRE sits still.

FATHER: He's coming, Pierre, he's coming.

PIERRE: The flies? Is it the flies? No!

The fire dies.

PIERRE: Hungry, hungry and cold.

FATHER: Pierre? Wait!

PIERRE: Make him go away!

FATHER: Don't leave me alone. We are his lambs. It's time for our celebration. Pierre?

PIERRE exits off into the dark.

FATHER: *(kneeling)* God, Creator and Defender of the human race. You who made man in your own image. Look on this, your servant who is assaulted by the cunning of unclean spirits. The primeval adversary, the ancient enemy of Earth, surrounds him with the horror of fear, paralyses his mind with darkness, strikes him with terror, agitates him with shaking and trembling—

The GHOST, a skeleton dressed in Black-Robe rags, enters carrying a glowing, bloody heart.

FATHER: Oh, Father, where have you been? I've been so lonely. I thought the darkness of this wilderness would never end.

The GHOST offers FATHER Noel the heart. Lightning and then thunder.

FATHER: Oh most holy— How long have I waited for you to say that! *(he takes the heart and takes a bite out of it)*

Scene Seven

In the same black night, the northern lights shift on the horizon. Star LILY sleeps beside an almost dead fire inside the women's wigwam, a drum at hand. Sky FEATHER and FLOOD Woman enter. Distant thunder.

FLOOD: Listen.

FEATHER: Is that thunder?

FLOOD: In the middle of winter? It doesn't sound right.

FEATHER: Look, there's no smoke.

The northern lights fade away.

FLOOD: Come on. I hope she's all right.

FLOOD Woman and Sky FEATHER enter the women's wigwam.

FEATHER: Hey, wake up. Wake up!

FLOOD: The fire's almost out.

LILY: *(opening her eyes)* Always looking out for me, aren't you?

FEATHER: Your hands are like ice.

LILY: I'm all right.

FEATHER: You could have died.

FLOOD: Sister, guess what? You can stop this. We've got something to eat. This fish— Listen to me!

LILY: There's no time.

FLOOD: No, come away from here.

FEATHER: It's colder in here than outside.

FLOOD: You've got to eat something.

LILY: I can't leave now. It's coming.

FEATHER: I'll get more wood.

LILY: No, don't bother. Fire won't do any good now.

FEATHER: Don't be silly. You're half frozen. And I'm not going to freeze with you. *(she gets the wood from just outside)*

FLOOD: What is it? What's going on?

LILY: I'm not sure.

FLOOD: Why are you laughing?

LILY: I haven't been hungry for days.

FLOOD: Did your helpers come to you? Do you know what's wrong?

FEATHER: That's better.

FLOOD: Will the men find game?

FEATHER: Nothing like a fire to get the colour back into you.

FLOOD: If the men came you could eat something.

LILY: You're hungry, aren't you? Here.

FEATHER: Where'd you get all these berries?

LILY: The Frenchman left them for me.

FEATHER: He didn't come in here, did he?

LILY: No, he's not stupid. Your baby's hungry. You should eat them. Go on, go ahead.

FLOOD: Go ahead.

FEATHER: I almost forgot how to chew.

FLOOD: I know what you mean.

FEATHER: Oh they're so sweet it hurts.

LILY: Your stomach's loud.

FEATHER: Have some.

FLOOD: Just a bite.

LILY: Only the baby should eat now.

FLOOD: I'm hungry!

Thunder closer by.

FEATHER: It's as loud as my stomach.

LILY: That's what it is. *(she plays a few beats on her drum, an answer to the thunder)* Another stomach rumbling.

FLOOD: What is it? You know what's wrong.

LILY: Listen to this. Listen. *(she plays her drum again, finds a rhythm)*

FEATHER: What are you talking about?

LILY: The hunger's too great now. We can't eat.

FLOOD: Sure we can! There's a fish cooking right now in our pot. And my mother won't wait.

FEATHER: We're all so hungry.

FLOOD: A big sturgeon floated up out of nowhere.

LILY: No. It isn't safe. We have to be clear. We'd only be feeding the hunger.

The thunder rumbles closer, a monstrous gut.

FEATHER: What are we going to do?

LILY: The cannibal spirit's coming.

FLOOD: I wish my uncle were here.

LILY: I'm going to try and fight it off.

FEATHER: You don't know what to do. You're a little girl.

LILY: You're going to look after me.

FLOOD: I don't know the songs well enough.

LILY: Just play what I showed you.

FEATHER: I should go find my mother. She can help.

LILY: There's no time for that. Here. Drink this. Both of you. Drink it.

FEATHER: It's awful.

FLOOD: How do you know this?

LILY: My helpers came. They promised me that tea will kill any hunger. It will keep your mind clear. Now you've got to drum for me.

FLOOD: I don't know...

LILY: Do it. Just like I did. Go on. That's right.

FLOOD Woman begins to drum. The northern lights reappear near the horizon.

FEATHER: What about me?

LILY: Keep the fire going. You were right. I would have died.

A flash of lightning almost overhead.

FEATHER: It's freezing again!

Star LILY begins singing along with the drum and closes her eyes. The northern lights drift across the snow. Sky FEATHER puts more sticks on the fire. The thunder approaches overhead. The northern lights surround the wigwam, a spectral palisade. More lightning and then the spectral blizzard begins.

Scene Eight

The spectral blizzard blows across the confusion of ice on Lake Nipissing and around a black rock island there in the night. Fire CLOUD enters, leading IRON Man and Thunder VOICE into the lee of the rock.

VOICE: Why are we stopping?

CLOUD: We'll rest here. The wind's shifted direction.

VOICE: Are we lost now?

IRON: This wind has no direction.

VOICE: What is this place?

IRON: Maybe it's that rock off the south island.

VOICE: So we've been going in the wrong direction all along?

The ice groans beneath their feet.

IRON: We've been going in a circle. It's not far if we cut across. Come on.

CLOUD: Wait. The current's strong there.

VOICE: It's been cold all winter. The ice'll be thick enough.

IRON: This wind could open it up.

CLOUD: We should stay in the shelter of the islands.

VOICE: It'll take forever.

CLOUD: You weren't in any hurry before.

VOICE: I didn't know we'd get lost.

CLOUD: Black Star told us to think about the women.

VOICE: That stupid old man? He couldn't take care of his own wife!

The blizzard pauses.

CLOUD: We had time to get home before the storm started.

VOICE: Come on, I'll lead the way.

CLOUD: But you had to feed your stomach.

VOICE: You didn't complain about my rabbit when it was in your mouth.

Fire CLOUD slaps Thunder VOICE.

CLOUD: I'm your father.

Thunder VOICE turns away.

CLOUD: Is this what the Black Robe teaches you? Look at me.

IRON: Is there any left? Any rabbit?

VOICE: Here. *(he takes the package of meat from his bag and throw it down)*

IRON: Let's finish it up before we go on. I could use a bite.

VOICE: I'll go on ahead.

CLOUD: Is my son a whining woman now?

VOICE: I won't make my mother a widow.

CLOUD: That's all she deserves who has no sons.

IRON: There's no time for this. Listen to me. Both of you. Think of your wives, your daughter, your sister. Think of them.

CLOUD: It's the hunger. The hunger's talking.

          An arrow flies from the rock and pierces Fire CLOUD through the heart and he falls dead.

VOICE: Father?

          The SECOND and THIRD Mohawks appear above them on the rock, bows drawn.

IRON: Look out!

VOICE: Help me with him!

IRON: It's no good. Leave him. Leave him!

          The SECOND and THIRD Mohawks fire two more arrows but IRON Man and Thunder VOICE avoid them, ducking below the rock.

VOICE: Where are they? Have they moved?

The THIRD Mohawk starts to clamber down out of sight. IRON Man peeks out. The SECOND Mohawk fires another arrow and IRON Man draws back.

VOICE: How did they get here?

The ice gives an unearthly howl and splits apart and Fire CLOUD's body slips into the water. The blizzard starts up again.

VOICE: My father! My father...

The shock of the splitting ice shook the THIRD Mohawk loose from the rock face and now he slips down almost on top of Thunder VOICE. IRON Man pulls Thunder VOICE back.

IRON: Look out!

Thunder VOICE falls onto his back on the ice. IRON Man jumps the THIRD Mohawk and they wrestle. The SECOND Mohawk shoots again, wounding IRON Man in the arm. The SECOND Mohawk gives a war whoop as the THIRD Mohawk pins IRON Man down. Thunder VOICE pulls the THIRD Mohawk off IRON Man. The THIRD Mohawk slides into the open water.

VOICE: Are you all right?

IRON: Careful. Careful!

The SECOND Mohawk screams in frustration and draws another arrow but a ball of green fire appears in the air in front of him and he stumbles back from it in terror.

VOICE: Iron Man! Iron Man, look!

The fire ball herds the SECOND Mohawk to the brink and he falls down the rock face into the open water. The fire ball explodes.

VOICE: Did you see that? Iron Man, did you see?

The ice groans and closes.

VOICE: What's going on?

IRON: Black Star's here somewhere.

VOICE: Black Star's here?

IRON: He said they'd come after the women.

BEAR: *(off)* Come on! This way! *(he enters out of the blizzard)*

VOICE: You know what happened?

BEAR: My father's trying to fight the blizzard.

VOICE: He's fighting the blizzard! My father's dead.

BEAR: We didn't know you were still out here.

VOICE: He's dead. The ice ate his body.

BEAR: Come on!

VOICE: What good is all that old man's medicine!

IRON: Where is he? Is he all right?

BEAR: He'll meet us by the next island. He's in his tent there.

VOICE: And this man here is wounded!

IRON: I'll be fine.

BEAR: We have to hurry. *(he exits)*

IRON: Come on. Come on, help me.

Thunder VOICE helps IRON Man to his feet and they follow BEAR off into the blizzard.

Scene Nine

The same black night, in the spectral blizzard PIERRE lies in the snow near the trail to the water hole. Another trail crosses it nearby. SAMUEL, armed with a knife, enters along the other trail, and seeing tracks, turns and finds PIERRE.

SAMUEL: Hey, wake up. What's wrong, little Father?

THISTLE: *(off, at a distance)* Frenchman! Frenchman, where are you?

SAMUEL: Pierre, where is he? Where's Father Noel?

PIERRE: Please. The flies...

SAMUEL: Where's the Black Robe?

THISTLE: *(off, nearer)* Frenchman, wait. Don't leave me.

SAMUEL: You're shivering.

PIERRE: Don't hurt me!

THISTLE: *(entering along the other trail, armed with a war club)* Frenchman, where are you?

PIERRE: Keep the flies away...

SAMUEL: Over here.

THISTLE: Why didn't you wait for me? I'm out of breath.

SAMUEL: I found the little Father.

THISTLE: The little cannibal? Be careful.

SAMUEL: It's all right.

THISTLE: Don't let him bite you!

SAMUEL: There's something wrong with him. He's cold as ice.

THISTLE: He's a cannibal. We have to kill him.

SAMUEL: He's not a cannibal.

THISTLE: Well tie him up. Tie him up then.

SAMUEL: Do you have a rope?

THISTLE: But he'll be strong when he wakes up.

SAMUEL: Where's Father Noel?

THISTLE: We have to burn him.

SAMUEL: Where is he?

PIERRE: Gone to hell!

SAMUEL: Look at me.

PIERRE: Good riddance.

THISTLE: Frenchman, what's he saying?

SAMUEL: He's making sense.

THISTLE: We should have gone for my daughter first.

SAMUEL: Hail Stone Woman's house was closer.

THISTLE: Why's he crying?

SAMUEL: Something happened to him.

THISTLE: Father Noel tried to eat him.

PIERRE: I want to go home.

SAMUEL: Little Father, why are you crying?

PIERRE: I want to go home! Let me go home!

THISTLE: Cannibals don't cry...

PIERRE: I wish I'd never come here.

SAMUEL: Pierre, look at me.

PIERRE: The devils are here. The devils!

SAMUEL: Look at me. What's wrong?

PIERRE: You were right.

SAMUEL: I was right?

PIERRE: There is no God.

SAMUEL: You were listening to me.

THISTLE: Frenchman, what's he saying?

SAMUEL: What did you see? Was it the Father? What was it? What was it?

PIERRE: That woman who lived over there?

SAMUEL: What about her? He's talking about Hail Stone Woman.

THISTLE: Where is she?

PIERRE: She ate a poison fish.

SAMUEL: She ate a poison fish?

PIERRE: It bewitched her. She told me so.

THISTLE: What's he saying?

SAMUEL: He's talking strange.

PIERRE: I came to visit her. I wanted her to give me something to eat. She turned into a snake!

THISTLE: What's wrong with him?

PIERRE: A giant snake, right before my eyes. See the tracks?

PIERRE is shaken by cramps.

SAMUEL: Pierre? Pierre, what's wrong?

PIERRE: Her face was crying. Her face. I saw her die then. Then her snake jaws swallowed her face up. She was so hungry.

SAMUEL: Pierre, look at me.

PIERRE: I was hungry. I'm sorry.

SAMUEL: There's nothing to be sorry about.

PIERRE: I ate the fish too. I ate the fish.

THISTLE: Look at his face.

PIERRE: I followed her, followed her over the hill to the water hole.

THISTLE: Look at his face!

PIERRE: She crawled in, went down there under the ice.

THISTLE: No! He's looking at me.

PIERRE: The ice swallowed her whole.

SAMUEL: He's afraid.

PIERRE: The ice was hungry.

SAMUEL: He's just afraid.

PIERRE: I don't want to be a snake. Please. Please...

THISTLE clubs PIERRE and splits his skull.

SAMUEL: Pierre? Pierre!

THISTLE: Close his eyes.

SAMUEL: What did you do that for?

THISTLE: He was crying...

SAMUEL: Give me that.

THISTLE: I put him out of his misery. We can burn him now.

SAMUEL: What are you talking about?

THISTLE: He was a cannibal. He ate Hail Stone Woman. He would
have eaten us next.

SAMUEL: He didn't eat her.

THISTLE: He didn't eat her? He would have eaten us. What did
he say then?

SAMUEL: Rest in peace, Little Father.

THISTLE: What did he say? Frenchman?

SAMUEL: It was all strange. He said Hail Stone Woman... I think he said she turned into a snake.

THISTLE: A snake?

SAMUEL: She ate a poisoned fish. And crawled down the water hole into the lake.

THISTLE: Those tracks! I thought it was a sleigh.

SAMUEL: No one's got a sleigh. Where are you going?

THISTLE: We can't stay here. We got to leave this island.

SAMUEL: The men will be back soon. We have to wait.

THISTLE: I wish we could burn him.

SAMUEL: We'll burn him. Bear took my flint with him. We'll have to get fire.

THISTLE: What about Flood Woman? What about the baby? Did he say anything?

SAMUEL: Come on.

SAMUEL and THISTLE exeunt in the direction of the Hail Stone Woman's house. PIERRE's body is a shadow in the snow.

Scene Ten

A distant dawning greys the blizzard. HAIL Stone Woman's wigwam is in disarray, its fire dead. North Star sleeps fitfully. FATHER Noel enters from the trees, the stick-cross in hand.

FATHER: Pierre! Pierre? Where are you...?

North Star wakes and whines.

FATHER: *(looking into the wigwam)* You missed the celebration. We must be ready for his resurrection. Who's there? *(entering the wigwam)* Forgive me. *(he falls to his knees)* I bring you news that will save your soul. Behold the cross of the Lord, let its enemies take flight.

A red glow starts bleeding into the blizzard. North Star starts crying.

FATHER: The lion of the tribe of Juda has conquered, the root of David, I exorcise thee, creature of wood, in the name of God the Father Almighty, and in the name of Jesus Christ, his son our Lord, and in the power of the Holy Ghost...

FATHER Noel puts down the cross and picks North Star up. North Star starts wailing. In the distance the unearthly howling of the ice.

FATHER: Who's there? Father?

FATHER Noel, carrying North Star, comes out of the wigwam.

FATHER: Father, is that you? Father, where are you? We're here. We're ready, Father. We're coming. Wait for us.

FATHER Noel, carrying a crying North Star, exits into the blood red blizzard.

END OF ACT TWO

ACT THREE

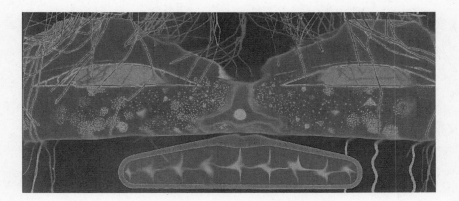

Scene One

An overcast dawn late in spring. Star LILY, playing her drum, Sky FEATHER, eight months pregnant, THISTLE and FLOOD Woman in a women's wigwam near the shore of Lake Temagami.

LILY: *(begins to chant)* We have lived through the winter, through hunger and wind, through fever and cold. Now we're grieving for those who have gone, the young and the old, for grandparents and parents, children and lovers—

FEATHER: *(to FLOOD Woman)* You're crying!

LILY: *(chanting, playing her drum)* —Now we are seeing the snow melting again, now we are tasting the sweet drops of sap—

FEATHER: This is a time to celebrate!

THISTLE: Be quiet!

LILY: *(chanting, playing her drum)* —now reaching out like the buds on branches. Soon we shall breathe the brightness of flowers, soon every day will be long.

THISTLE: 'Every day will be long.' That was good.

LILY: Not as good as Black Star.

THISTLE: He'll be better in time to sing the summer song.

FLOOD: Don't look at me. I can't help missing my mother, my baby...brother...

FEATHER: You don't see me whining. My father—

THISTLE: Stop it. Both of you. This is for the song.

THISTLE hands Star LILY a small pouch of tobacco. FLOOD Woman and Sky FEATHER also hand Star LILY pouches.

FEATHER: You don't see your sister here making with the tears.

FLOOD: Why don't you cry? What's wrong with you? Don't you care?

LILY: I care. I'm just trying to—

FLOOD: My mother loved you. She didn't throw you out of our house. She treated you like one of us.

LILY: Sure, she was scared of my mother's ghost.

FLOOD: She loved you. She gave you your share.

LILY: My father loves me.

THISTLE: Stop this! Stop it now. We're here for the song.

FEATHER: The song's over.

THISTLE: My husband died. The Iroquois killed my husband. Do you hear me crying? Saying his name? He's on another journey now. He's got other things to think about. You're supposed to be sisters. Your father wants you to be sisters. *(she gets to her feet, gets more wood for the fire)* Think about him. What about him?

FEATHER: How's he doing, your father?

LILY: No good.

FLOOD: He just stares at the fire.

LILY: No good at all.

FEATHER: It's all right.

LILY: He won't take my medicines.

THISTLE: No one should have to see that.

FEATHER: No one should have to do that. Don't talk about it.

FLOOD: It's all he talks about. Chasing the cannibal across the ice, slipping,falling down.

LILY: The ice all cracking up when the storm caught up to them.

FEATHER: I don't want to hear this again. *(she gets to her feet)*

FLOOD: But he thought the baby was going to be all right. That's what he says.

LILY: 'I thought he was going to be all right.'

THISTLE: My son and Bear were out ahead there. They'd cut off the cannibal's escape.

FEATHER: I'm going back to the camp. *(she leaves the wigwam, leaving the flap open, but stops just out of hearing)*

LILY: But the Black Robe put the baby down on the ice.

FLOOD: Left him there and ran away.

LILY: Singing those songs of his.

THISTLE: About the end of the world.

FLOOD: My father headed over to him. He thought he was going to be all right. You were there then, weren't you?

THISTLE: We caught up to them. The Frenchman got there first.

LILY: The poor man!

THISTLE: He didn't know what to do. The baby tried to bite him!

FLOOD: My father says North Star's eyes were like fires. He was grinding his new teeth.

LILY: Chewing the tips off his own fingers.

THISTLE: I knew what was wrong soon as I saw that.

FLOOD: My poor father.

THISTLE: His only son. I offered to do it.

LILY: No.

THISTLE: It was the only thing to do.

LILY: It was up to him to do it.

THISTLE: The Frenchman didn't know what was going on.

LILY: My father killed the little cannibal himself.

FLOOD: The baby's eyes were little fires.

THISTLE: We had to burn the body.

FLOOD: That's all he remembers. That's all.

THISTLE: I'm cold.

FLOOD: He shouldn't stare at the fire so much. *(she gets to her feet, reaches to close the flap)* I'll get more wood.

FEATHER: Are you finished? *(she comes back in)* I thought it was going to rain finally.

THISTLE: You're shivering.

FEATHER: I didn't want to go back there. I don't know those Sturgeon River women. All they talk about are the Iroquois.

THISTLE: They're right to worry. We got to keep moving north.

LILY: Maybe Black Star will make my father medicine.

FEATHER: The Frenchman says Black Star's still weak.

THISTLE: He should be better by now.

FEATHER: But his medicines aren't working. He's getting old.

THISTLE: His son should be helping him.

LILY: Some thing's can't be helped.

THISTLE: Where is he this time?

FLOOD: Bear went this morning with my husband and the men from Sturgeon River.

THISTLE: That Frenchman can't help anybody.

FLOOD: They're looking to see where the Iroquois are.

LILY: Bear and your brother looking to kill Iroquois?

FEATHER: If they don't kill each other first!

THISTLE: You should sing against the Iroquois again.

LILY: They won't come after us here.

FEATHER: We're out of their way now. They've got all our beaver.

FLOOD: She's tired, too.

THISTLE: A young girl like you!

LILY: Some things can't be helped.

THISTLE: That's all right. Eat. Build up your strength. You don't talk about it.

FEATHER: The Frenchman says the Iroquois are going after the people on the Ottawa now. We don't matter anymore.

FLOOD: You kept them away from us before. That was good. They couldn't find the island.

LILY: When the cannibal was taking North Star! *(she starts crying)*

FLOOD: No. You helped us. Don't say his name.

THISTLE: We shouldn't have asked you to do this today. It's too soon.

LILY: No. Today's the day to do it. Today's the right day.

FEATHER: I wish the sun would shine. I wish it would rain.

THISTLE: It's so dry. Winter stays too long up here.

FEATHER: The flowers are already out at home.

LILY: And the lake here! So deep, you can't see the bottom.

THISTLE: You don't want to see what lives down there. You'd be sick as Black Star is. We're not made for such things.

FEATHER: Maybe he's not made for such things. You said he was getting better. She's been spending a lot of time with him.

THISTLE: Well his son just leaves him alone.

LILY: A woman needs to take care of a man.

THISTLE: Show respect. I'm a widow.

FEATHER: A widow shouldn't be alone with that man.

FLOOD: Remember my aunt, his first wife?

THISTLE: Don't talk about it.

FEATHER: Mother, he's dangerous.

THISTLE: He saved our lives. He brought the thunder awake in winter, didn't he? He broke the ice and drowned the cannibal Father.

FEATHER: You're not a Christian anymore?

THISTLE: I never was. Not really.

> *Distant thunder.*

Scene Two

Thunder and the rain begins. Later the same overcast morning, the WARRIOR shelters under a lean-to on the shore of the Sturgeon River.

VOICE: (*off*) Hurry up, little 'old man'.

BEAR: (*off*) We're almost there.

> *The WARRIOR comes down to the shore.*

VOICE: (*off*) Hurry up!

> *BEAR and Thunder VOICE enter by canoe along the river, paddling to shore.*

BEAR: You can dry out by the fire.

VOICE: It's coming down harder.

BEAR: Stop complaining. You can't get any wetter than you are now.

WARRIOR: What have you seen, friends? *(he helps them beach the canoe)*

VOICE: Drowned camp fires.

WARRIOR: How many?

VOICE: Where's your father gone?

WARRIOR: They got a young moose. They've taken it back for the women.

VOICE: We're at war here! What if we'd come back with Iroquois on our trail! *(he goes to the fire and shelters under the lean-to)* Where's the tea?

BEAR: Two different places just below the rapids.

WARRIOR: That's a long way from here.

BEAR: It looks like they've gone, friend.

VOICE: This piss is worse than what you make.

BEAR: He talks too much sometimes.

The unearthly howling in the distance.

VOICE: What is that?

WARRIOR: I don't know. Some of the smaller lakes are still frozen.

VOICE: The ice at home never breaks like that.

BEAR: The lakes are deep here.

VOICE: I'm going to dry out. *(he lies down in the shelter)*

WARRIOR: There's some dried fish there. Help yourself.

VOICE: They could have left some of the moose.

WARRIOR: You rest too. I'll look after your canoe. We'll follow the others when the rain lets up.

Less rain for a moment.

BEAR: The rain should melt the last of the ice away. *(he goes to the lean-to and eats)* You want some help?

WARRIOR: You rest. I slept all night.

The WARRIOR unloads the canoe and turns it upside down against the rain. Lightning and more thunder. BEAR lies down. The WARRIOR puts the load into the canoe's shelter. FATHER Noel, dressed in rags, entirely cannibal now, enters, rising up out of the water and stepping up behind the WARRIOR. The WARRIOR hears him, draws his knife and turns, but stumbles back in terror, knocking the canoe right-side up. FATHER Noel grabs the knife, slits the WARRIOR's throat and throws the body into the canoe. The rain starts to pour. FATHER Noel climbs into the canoe, pushes off and paddles into the rain and an exit.

BEAR: *(sitting up)* Hey what's taking so long?

VOICE: Be quiet.

BEAR: He'll get all wet. Hey—Look. Look!

VOICE: What?

BEAR: He's gone!

VOICE: He's gone?

BEAR: He took the canoe too.

VOICE: What kind of joke is this?

BEAR: Is that him?

VOICE: Come on!

BEAR: Hey, Loud One, what do you think you're doing? We can't catch him.

VOICE: I think we can.

BEAR: Running along the river?

VOICE: He's going against the current.

BEAR: Will we fly over the rocks?

VOICE: Everybody knows the Sturgeon River people are slow. Rocks in his head.

BEAR: I thought you were related to them.

VOICE: I'll teach him to joke with us.

BEAR: I think he already knows how.

VOICE: Either use your old man's mouth to swallow the rain or shut it up and get move on. Come on!

Thunder VOICE and BEAR exeunt, running along the shore.

Scene Three

Later the same day, thunder in the distance, Black STAR sleeps beside a low fire in a wigwam near the shore of Lake Temagami. SAMUEL sits with him, watching out the doorway. THISTLE enters, comes to the wigwam.

THISTLE: How is he?

SAMUEL: Still asleep.

THISTLE: I brought you some berries. They got frozen but they're good if you eat them right away.

SAMUEL: I'll give them to him soon as he wakes up.

THISTLE: Frenchman. Why do you stay here?

SAMUEL: For the berries.

THISTLE: You could starve here. We don't have wine here. The Iroquois would kill you first.

SAMUEL: They won't come now.

THISTLE: You can't be a man here. You don't understand things.

SAMUEL: I'm a child now, learning to be a man.

THISTLE: No one will be a wife to a child.

SAMUEL: A child doesn't need a wife. What he needs is a mother who brings him berries.

THISTLE: One son's enough. This old man, the boy, they're teaching you dangerous things.

SAMUEL: I'm learning wonderful things.

THISTLE: You could die, and there's no Black Robes here to baptise you.

SAMUEL: The world's full of spirits. I don't have to die for life to be everlasting.

STAR: *(waking up suddenly)* Boy? Where is he?

SAMUEL: What is it?

STAR: Where's my son?

SAMUEL: He's looking out for Iroquois.

STAR: They won't come now.

THISTLE: You want some tea?

STAR: The one who made their medicine's dead.

SAMUEL: But something's wrong.

STAR: The Black Robe.

THISTLE: What about him?

STAR: He isn't gone.

SAMUEL: He drowned.

THISTLE: You killed him. I saw the lake open up and swallow him.

STAR: The cannibal didn't drown.

THISTLE: But cannibals can't live after the winter. Their hunger melts away.

SAMUEL: Father Noel was always hungry.

STAR: This isn't about banic.

THISTLE: Even before winter came he was hungry.

STAR: He never was hungry for bodies. He's been waiting in the lake.

SAMUEL: What for?

STAR: Waiting deep down where no one could find him.

THISTLE: How do you know this?

STAR: He's been holding onto me, onto us, all this time.

THISTLE: Is that why you're still so weak?

STAR: That's why I'm weak. And why the spring is late. Ask the people who live here where their dreaming place is.

SAMUEL: But what's going on?

STAR: Ask them if I can set my tent up there. Go on. Hurry.

SAMUEL exits.

THISTLE: Why do you know this now?

STAR: He's come up for air.

THISTLE: What else? What else has he come up for?

STAR: Your grandchild. He wants the spirit from it before it's born.

THISTLE: That's what he's hungry for.

STAR: I think that's what he's wanted all along.

THISTLE: What can I do?

STAR: I need more water.

THISTLE: What about your son?

STAR: Find him and my niece. They have to take me to that dreaming place and sing for me like I did for them last summer.

   THISTLE exits. Black STAR builds the fire up, then starts to sort through his herbs and roots. Sky FEATHER enters and comes to the wigwam.

FEATHER: Have you seen my mother? I need my mother.

STAR: What's wrong?

FEATHER: I need to pee, all right? I need her now. Is she with Star Lily?

STAR: *(coming out of the wigwam)* Wait.

FEATHER: She's at the lake, isn't she? Fishing with your niece.

STAR: Girl, come back here. Is it time? Wait here for her! Girl!

   Sky FEATHER exits.

STAR: Stay here! Don't go down there.

   Black STAR falls to his knees in the drizzle, catching his breath. The thunder approaches.

Scene Four

Late in the grey day, the shaking tent has been set up in the dreaming place high on a rock face. The rain has stopped but fog now is rising up to the heights. Star LILY sits under a lean-to beside the tent tending the fire. IRON Man enters up the slope and approaches her.

IRON: Hey! Where is he?

LILY: He's on his way.

IRON: Do you need anything?

LILY: We're all ready.

IRON: Is it true? What the Frenchman said about the Black Robe?

LILY: Have some tea.

IRON: The Sturgeon River People...

LILY: What about them?

IRON: They packed up and left soon as they heard.

LILY: They've run away. They're not stupid.

IRON: The people who live here have gone too.

LILY: It's been getting colder all day.

IRON: What's taking him so long?

LILY: See for yourself.

SAMUEL enters out of the fog, using the oak stick to balance with, carrying Black STAR on his back.

IRON: Can I help?

SAMUEL: I'm fine.

IRON: I'm here to help.

STAR: Put me down.

IRON: Are you so weak?

LILY: The medicine's ready.

STAR: There's some for each of us.

IRON: You knew I'd be here?

STAR: You're a warrior.

LILY: This one's making a face!

STAR: There's some for you too. Drink up.

SAMUEL: I guess I had worse in my mouth when I was Christian.

IRON: This is true then.

STAR: All this time he's been inside me like a worm.

IRON: What will I do?

STAR: Take the stick. It protected me before. The trees want spring to come too.

IRON: I will sing my songs to them.

STAR: The girl and her mother are in the women's house. The cannibal's looking for them. You have to keep him away until my helpers wake up.

LILY: Keep your spirit strong.

STAR: You'll feel hungry and cold. Lonely and tired. Thirsty and afraid.

LILY: You might hear someone crying for help. Don't go. Remember your song.

SAMUEL: I'll go with him.

STAR: No, my son's not here. Someone has to play the drum for her while she sings.

SAMUEL: But I'm a Frenchman.

STAR: Any child can play the drum.

IRON Man gets up to leave and stops to listen.

LILY: What is it?

IRON: All day I've been hearing my son's voice, crying somewheres off in the woods. I think he's gone to sleep now. *(he exits into the fog)*

Black STAR goes into the tent, Star LILY feeds the fire, SAMUEL tries out the drum. Thunder in the distance. The fog is rising.

Scene Five

On the night the canoe is beached along the rocky shore of the Sturgeon River. Thunder VOICE enters out of the spectral fog.

VOICE: Come on. Hurry up or I'll leave you.

BEAR: *(off)* Wait.

VOICE: He never rests. Neither will we.

BEAR: *(off)* I know where we are.

VOICE: Or do you want him to get away?

BEAR: *(entering)* No, listen—

VOICE: I'm not listening to you anymore.

BEAR: Just listen. Do you hear?

VOICE: What? Is he singing to you?

BEAR: Close your mouth for once.

VOICE: Rapids!

BEAR: Come on. Down here!

VOICE: You're wasting my time.

BEAR: Look. We're at the last bend before the rapids.

VOICE: Does that mean something?

BEAR: We're back at the deep lake.

VOICE: Are you sure? How did we come so far?

BEAR: Come here!

VOICE: How does he keep going?

BEAR: See.

VOICE: It's the canoe.

BEAR: That's where he came ashore.

VOICE: If we cut up through these woods, we should be able to catch up. Now where are you going?

BEAR: I want to check the canoe first.

VOICE: Have you lost your knife again? I'll leave you here.

BEAR: Go ahead. I'll catch up.

VOICE: All right. Hurry. So what do you see?

BEAR: There's a lot of blood.

VOICE: Did you say blood?

BEAR: It's him. Your Sturgeon River relative.

VOICE: Let me see.

BEAR: His heart.

VOICE: Who would do this to him?

BEAR: Someone's been eating him.

VOICE: A cannibal? A cannibal!

BEAR: He was a good man.

VOICE: We've been chasing a cannibal all this time!

BEAR: You're as brave as you are smart.

VOICE: Shut your mouth.

BEAR: Come this way. I know these trees.

BEAR and Thunder VOICE exit into the fog.

Scene Six

In the night, in the fog, somewhere among the rocks and trees near the women's wigwam, IRON Man keeps watch, branch in hand. FLOOD Woman enters.

FLOOD: Father?

IRON: Where'd you come from?

FLOOD: I've brought you a blanket.

IRON: It's like winter all over again.

FLOOD: The path is all icy.

IRON: I must have fallen asleep.

FLOOD: It's all right. It's late.

IRON: I can feel him.

FLOOD: He's close by.

IRON: You better go back.

FLOOD: I've been thinking about my mother.

IRON: Think about Sky Feather.

FLOOD: My mother's spirit is walking a path to the west. She's carrying my brother, carrying his spirit in her arms. My aunt's there to show them the way.

IRON: Your aunt?

FLOOD: The one who married Black Star. She's like she was before she was killed. They all are. They don't need flesh and pain anymore, just each other. My aunt's tongue is back in her mouth like a bird in a nest in spring.

IRON: You believe that?

FLOOD: One day we'll get to hear how she sings.

IRON: I hope it's true. You better go back now. Go on.

FLOOD: It's no use.

IRON: What do you mean? Why are you crying?

FLOOD: Sky Feather...

IRON: Look at me.

FLOOD: She's dead, father.

IRON: What are you talking about?

FLOOD: The baby, it came early.

IRON: It came early?

FLOOD: The baby came early and Sky Feather died.

IRON: This is true?

FLOOD: It hurt to hear her crying. She was so afraid.

IRON: Not again.

FLOOD: There was so much blood. It wouldn't stop.

IRON: What about the baby?

FLOOD: I think it was dead.

IRON: It was dead?

FLOOD: It felt cold.

IRON: What am I doing here!

FLOOD: Thistle wrapped it up in a blanket. She was sad. She
         was singing to it.
         Hush, now, hush, baby boy.
         Go to sleep—

IRON: Come on.

FLOOD: I tried to tell her about the path of the spirits.

IRON: Show me the way.

FLOOD: It's the women's house. You could get hurt.

IRON: Show me the way!

FLOOD Woman and IRON Man exit into the fog.

Scene Seven

*In the night, in the spectral fog, a terrified THISTLE enters over the rocks, carry-
ing the bundled baby. She changes direction once and again, then trips and falls
but holds the baby safe. She catches her breath, listening, then starts to get up.*

VOICE: *(off)* Come on!

         THISTLE gives a cry.

BEAR: *(off)* Wait!

VOICE: *(off)* What now?

BEAR: *(off)* There's someone here.

VOICE: *(off)* Where are you?

BEAR: *(entering)* This way, Loud One. Hurry.

VOICE: *(off)* Who is it?

BEAR: It's your mother.

VOICE: *(entering)* What? Where are you?

BEAR: What's going on? What are you doing here? Look at me. What's wrong with you? She's shaking.

VOICE: Mother? Mother, answer.

BEAR: It's a baby.

VOICE: Mother, it's me. Look at me.

BEAR: A baby girl. It's all blue.

THISTLE: My little boy?

BEAR: A blue baby.

THISTLE: My little baby! Oh son...

VOICE: Mother, what's going on? Whose baby is this? Whose baby?

THISTLE: The cannibal's...

VOICE: Look at me. What are you talking about?

THISTLE: The Black Robe. He came back. He came back for the baby.

BEAR: He's the cannibal?

THISTLE: He was hungry after all this time. He was hungry.

VOICE: All this time?

THISTLE: All this time in the lake. He started eating her body and singing his songs.

BEAR: Whose body?

THISTLE: Your sister.

VOICE: What about her?

THISTLE: She died.

VOICE: My sister died?

THISTLE: She died because he was near.

BEAR: Where is he now? Where's the Black Robe?

THISTLE: He's still with her. He's still with her.

BEAR: Look at me. Where are they?

VOICE: Don't cry, mother. Tell us where they are.

BEAR: The women's house?

THISTLE: He said he wanted to pray for her. He asked me to celebrate with him. Celebrate the end of the world. He took out his knife.

VOICE: Mother, look at me.

THISTLE: I took the baby away and ran. Don't let him find me. Don't let him find us.

VOICE: Which way to the house?

THISTLE: You shouldn't go there.

BEAR: Which way is it?

THISTLE: You know how to take care?

BEAR: We'll be all right.

THISTLE: You do?

BEAR: I'll be all right.

THISTLE: It's over there, across the creek.

BEAR: Give me your knife.

VOICE: I'm coming with you. My sister—

BEAR: No, it's too late.

THISTLE: It's too late. Too late. Don't cry, little boy.

BEAR: No, look after the baby. Take her to your sister-in-law.

VOICE: It's dead.

BEAR: Don't be so sure. I think she's just lost her way. Maybe Star Lily will be able to help her. Hurry. *(he exits over the rocks)*

VOICE: Come on, mother.

THISTLE: We're not going back there?

VOICE: We're going to Star Lily's house.

THISTLE: She's too young to name a baby.

Thunder VOICE and THISTLE, still carrying the bundled baby, exeunt through the fog.

Scene Eight

In the night, in the spectral fog, fire light flickers through the door of the women's wigwam. BEAR enters and sneaks up around the back of the wigwam, knife drawn. FATHER Noel comes out, gory-faced, sniffing the air. BEAR jumps him and they fight.

IRON: *(off)* What's that? Do you hear?

FLOOD: *(off)* Look. Look over there.

              In the distance, a humming noise and the mist begins to disperse. BEAR loses his knife, is weakening. IRON Man, with his stick, and FLOOD Woman enter.

IRON: Come on!

              IRON Man runs forward as FATHER Noel pins BEAR down and picks up the knife. The humming is getting closer, greater. IRON Man knocks the knife out of FATHER Noel's hand with the stick. FATHER Noel leaps to his feet, coming after IRON Man. FATHER Noel yanks the stick away, knocking IRON Man to the ground with it. FLOOD Woman screams and leaps onto FATHER Noel's back. BEAR picks up his knife while FATHER Noel drops the stick, shakes FLOOD Woman off. Before FATHER Noel can chase her, IRON Man tackles him around the waist and BEAR grabs him around the neck, slitting his throat. The humming is loud, hovering. FATHER Noel falls quivering, bleeding to the ground, letting out the unearthly howl, and BEAR, IRON Man and FLOOD Woman retreat in terror. FATHER Noel starts to get up but then the humming descends, a cloud of black flies that eats the flesh off his bones, turning him into a physical facsimile of the GHOST. He stumbles, screams. FLOOD Woman grabs the stick, goes to the wigwam and lights the stick's end from the fire there and returns to hit through the cloud of flies at the dancing skeleton and break it in half. The skeleton falls back into the wigwam and everything, even the black flies, goes up in green flame. The mist is gone and stars rise in the sky.

Scene Nine

The last quarter moon in a clear predawn sky, the horizon a yellow band of light. Three canoes adrift on Lake Temagami. The middle canoe holds THIS-TLE, Star LILY, rocking the bundled baby, and IRON Man. The canoe to one side holds Thunder VOICE and FLOOD Woman, the canoe to the other side holds BEAR and SAMUEL.

THISTLE: How is she?

LILY: She wants to be here. She wants to have her life. But she's lost. It's so dark there. And there's so much death here. She can't see where we are.

THISTLE: We'll be out of this shadow soon.

IRON: It's going to be warm today. Even north of here.

THISTLE: That's where everyone else has gone.

BEAR: What did she say to you?

SAMUEL: 'You don't have to stay here. Now that the ice is gone, other Frenchmen aren't far away.'

BEAR: What did you tell her?

SAMUEL: 'How can I leave now? His father's dead. I have to learn to help him.'

FLOOD: What's wrong?

VOICE: My mother. She keeps talking about the Black Robe.

FLOOD: Don't talk about him.

VOICE: That's what I said to her. 'Don't mention his name.' But she said he told her a story once.

FLOOD: Just once!

BEAR: You didn't tell her?

SAMUEL: That your father asked you to smother him, that you had to burn his body yourself?

BEAR: No one needs to know.

FLOOD: Forget it. He's gone now for good.

VOICE: She said it was about a people who had to leave a place where they were being bewitched.

FLOOD: He was mocking her.

VOICE: I think so too. They wandered in a place without trees for years before they got home.

FLOOD: No such place exists.

SAMUEL: The old man had all those tongues in his bag.

BEAR: They belonged to the men who killed my grandfather, my mother.

SAMUEL: All those tongues! I didn't think there'd be so many. Did we have to burn and his birch barks and furs?

BEAR: You like it dangerous.

SAMUEL: A cloud of black flies flew out of his body, out of his body into the fire!

BEAR: Stop smiling. My father's dead.

SAMUEL: You first.

LILY: You're the oldest one of us now.

THISTLE: It's up to you to name her.

IRON: What use is it? Is she going to live?

LILY: What will you call her?

IRON: Broken Moon.

LILY: A baby with nothing to carry from this world to the next. No blanket, no bowl. No name.

IRON: How's Broken Moon?

LILY: And people are walking past her. It's the path of the spirits. Don't go!

THISTLE: Her parents are gone that way.

LILY: Don't go...

IRON: Come on, everyone! We're not getting anywhere like this!

They begin to paddle north. There is light overhead.

LILY: Broken Moon, come this way! This way!

BEAR: My father said we have to always be on guard.

LILY: You are light as a feather in the blackness. Don't be afraid.

BEAR: He said the cannibals will always be after us here.

LILY: She wants to dance. And the dead are holding a dance.

BEAR: He said we've got to go away from here way far up north.

LILY: They're laughing and drumming, playing pipes far sweeter than any we will ever play.

BEAR: We've got to travel way beyond the camp of our old trading partners, the Cree.

LILY: If she dances with them, she'll never find her way back.

BEAR: We've got to go to a place where the lake tastes of salt.

LILY: No, baby, no! Here we have heads and arms.

BEAR: Then we'll turn towards where the sun sets.

LILY: Here we have scars and memories.

The GHOST, a skeleton dressed in Black-Robe rags, enters walking on the water again, following them, carrying the stick-cross now in flames.

BEAR: There's a place there, we will reach it before winter.

LILY: It's strange how they dance.

BEAR: The cannibals won't get there for years.

LILY: There are parts of their bodies missing.

BEAR: He said they'll eat the sun out of the sky.

LILY: But their dancing is happier than any we'll ever do with our bodies that are whole.

BEAR: But he said the sun will grow back again.

LILY: They dance all night long.

BEAR: He said that's when we'll return home.

LILY: They've overcome death.

BEAR: That's when we'll drive them and their Iroquois back across the great bright lake.

LILY: Broken Moon, come this way. We love you.

BEAR: It's a place of the living.

LILY: She's turning this way. She can't see us. She only sees a column of blue fire.

BEAR: Do you know what my father said?

LILY: Broken Moon, don't be afraid. This way! Come on, this way!

BEAR: He said the baby will wake up there.

LILY: Soon you'll step into the fire. Soon you'll step into your flesh.

They paddle into the brightness and an exit. The GHOST turns to follow them but then the sun rises and he disappears in the light.

THE END

THE AUTHOR THANKS THE DEPARTMENT OF ENGLISH AND THE SCHOOL OF DRAMATIC ART OF THE FACULTY OF ARTS AT THE UNIVERSITY OF WINDSOR AND THE ONTARIO ARTS COUNCIL THROUGH CAHOOTS THEATRE PROJECTS FOR THEIR SUPPORT OF THE DEVELOPMENT OF THIS PLAY. AND FOR THEIR COURAGE, HE THANKS COLIN TAYLOR AND LISA SODA.

BRÉBEUF'S GHOST

DANIEL DAVID MOSES